WEEKEND!

A Menu Cookbook for Relaxed Entertaining

Edited by Deborah Balmuth

Cover and text design by Meredith Maker

Cover photograph by A. Blake Gardner

Text production by Wanda Harper Joyce

Line drawings by Brigita Fuhrmann

Indexed by Word•a•bil•i•ty

Printed in the United States by Capital City Press

First Printing, September 1994

Library of Congress Cataloging-in-Publication Data

Stovel, Edith, 1940–
    Weekend! : a menu cookbook for relaxed entertaining / Edith Stovel and Pamela Wakefield
        p.   cm.
    Includes index.
    ISBN 0-88266-848-X—ISBN 0-88266-847-1 (pbk.)
    1. Entertaining. 2. Cookery. 3. Menus. I. Wakefield, Pamela, 1940–   . II. Title
TX731.S76 1994
642—dc20   94-7937
                                          CIP

WEEKEND!

A Menu Cookbook for Relaxed Entertaining

Edith Stovel
and
Pamela Wakefield

A Storey Publishing Book

Storey Communications, Inc.
Schoolhouse Road
Pownal, Vermont 05261

Pictured on cover: "A Weekend in Ski Country" (see pages 38–47), Friday Arrival Supper. Spaghetti with Chunky Tomato Mushroom Sauce, Sautéed Broccoli and Garlic, Focaccia with Sage and Rosemary, and Fresh Fruit.

RECIPE CREDITS FOR *WEEKEND!*

Recipe on page 34 from *Come On In! Recipes from the Junior League of Jackson, Mississippi,* P.O. Box 4709, Jackson, MS 39296. (601) 948-2357.

Recipe on page 52 from *Fresh Approach* by Susan R. Simpkins.

Recipe on page 70 from *The Florida Cookbook: A Lighter Look at Southern Cooking* by The Orlando Sentinel ((add name of authors per permission)).

Recipe on page 72 from *The Food Pharmacy Guide to Good Eating* by Jean Carper. Copyright © 1991 by Jean Carper. Used by permission of Bantam Books, a division of Bantam Doubleday Dell Publishing Group, Inc.

Recipe on page 98 from *The Frog Commissary Cookbook* by Steve Poses and Rebecca Roller. Copyright © 1985 by The Commissary, Inc. Used by permission of Doubleday, a division of Bantam Doubleday Dell Publishing Group, Inc.

Recipe on page 144 from *Good Friends, Great Dinners* by Susan Costner. Copyright © 1987 by Susan Costner. Reprinted by permission of Crown Publishers, Inc.

Recipe on page 199 from *Eating Well Magazine.*

This book is dedicated to our mothers

Beatrice McCoy
and
Patricia Clapp

The Cook and the Writer

CONTENTS

ACKNOWLEDGMENTS

We are deeply grateful to Storey Communications, Inc. for supporting this project. I especially want to thank Gwen Steege, senior editor, great cook, and dear friend for her wisdom and advice on all matters; John and Martha Storey for being the wonderful people they are with the vision, determination, and work ethic to create such a dynamic, exciting company as SCI and for their enthusiastic encouragement of my new career; and Deborah Balmuth for her warm support, thoughtful and careful editing, and intelligent suggestions. *E.S.*

Many friends and family members have inspired, advised, contributed, tested, tasted, chopped, blended, and sampled with us. Thank you: John Anderson, Dink Asano, the Berry Women, Julie Cohen, Jan Cowell, Pat Dimauro, Sarah Gall, Julie Jackson, Sandy Jorling, Stacey Joyce, Jean Langway, Susan and Dennis McCoy, Craig Smith, Larrie and Rocky Rockwell, Andy and Stuart Shatken of The Store at Five Corners, Martha Storey, Lennie Stovel, the Wadsworth's staff, and Tana Yarano.

Our children, Wendy and Chip Davis, Meg and Jezz Holland, Liza and Jamie Peck, Kate Stovel, and J.B. Wakefield, have not only been constructive critics and tasters, but also enthusiastic and supportive. We love and thank them all. And to our two giant fans, Jack and Bill, we are most grateful. *E.S. & P.W.*

PREFACE

Weekend, the frosting of the week, often brings a sigh of relief! It offers a change of pace, a chance to catch up on chores, relax over coffee, read the Sunday paper, and work around the yard. We relish the chance to enjoy a leisurely meal, go out, run, hike, see friends, and slow down. The anticipation is glorious, the possibilities endless. One of the nicest ways to enjoy weekends is to entertain friends, yet, even with good friends and favorite family members, weekend entertaining can be stressful. However, we've found that with some advance planning, shared meal preparation, and built-in relaxation time, the weekend can be truly refreshing.

The Wakefields and Stovels have spent many weekends together over the years, growing up and older together. In addition to sharing a great affection for one another, our families have enjoyed a mutual love of food and food preparation. Pam always presents us with inspiring and delicious combinations of ingredients. With seeming ease, she creates an atmosphere of comfort, relaxation, and fun. Not only is the food great and the preparation shared, but the best conversations seem to take place in the kitchen, over the cutting board. We always feel well cared for and certainly well fed. *E.S.*

DeeDee and I go back a long way — back, in fact to the days of marshmallow and jello salads. We have always shared an interest in food. DeeDee is just plain good at food. She has been reading and writing about it for years and her enthusiasm is contagious. I have never heard her describe a dish without wanting to slip into the kitchen and try it out myself. She has put a priority on making healthy food exciting and exciting food healthy.

My favorite recipes are those that depend more on an interesting combination of ingredients than on my ability to bone a duck or whip up a galantine. Friends and family should feel that their visits have been carefully planned for and happily anticipated. Food is a way of making that happen. This is easier to achieve for a lunch or a dinner than for a weekend, of course, but that is why we are so pleased with this book. We have done the planning, so you can enjoy the weekend, and your guests will depart feeling refreshed and pampered. *P.W.*

This book is dedicated to friendship and the nurturing of friendship through shared meals and times together. It is for those who want to break bread with friends and don't mind sharing the preparations with those they care about. It is for those who love good food that is attractively presented, is delicious and nutritious to eat, and doesn't require endless hours in the kitchen.

INTRODUCTION

This weekend menu cookbook grew out of years of spending weekends at each other's homes, planning and preparing meals together, and always seeking to fit in activities with children, other guests, spouses, and each other as well. The goal of this book is for the cook to enjoy the weekend. We have done the thinking and planning that go into food preparation so that you and your guests have more time to do the things you most want to do, whether it be cooking, skiing, hiking, relaxing — or any combination. Not only are the menus planned to be delicious, well-balanced, and appealing, but the steps to achieving these meals are all planned out for you. A little advance preparation can go a long way. We give you a list of things you can do the week before your guests arrive, distributed throughout the week to accommodate a busy work schedule. And for the weekend itself, we've provided a work plan to lead you step-by-step through the meal preparation, with suggestions for small cooking chores that can be assigned to willing guests.

Some weekend guests arrive Friday, some Saturday; some stay one night, some for several days. We have included menus to accommodate these possibilities — from a short three-meal weekend to a long seven-meal weekend — and everything in between. Some menus will appeal to large extended families with many young children, others are tailored for young urban adults, and there are options for a variety of other groups. We created some weekend plans for celebrating special holidays and family events, others for enjoying a special activity, and a few for weekends spent just relaxing with friends. The recipes combine our family specialties, some original creations, new discoveries, and adaptations of old favorites. The twenty weekends we've selected clearly reflect the gatherings and celebrations that have been meaningful to us, and the seasonal cycles of the northeastern United States region where we live. But we're sure that you'll find them very adaptable to the weekend events you enjoy most, and the seasonal variations of your home region. We had a great time planning and preparing the food for each weekend, and in the process figuring out the best way to make everything go smoothly. We hope this book is useful to you, and that you have many funfilled weekends with it.

Strategies for Making the Weekend Run Smoothly

One of the difficulties of meal planning for weekend guests is the sheer number of meals required and the prospect of constant food preparation. To ease this strain, we have included self-service breakfasts and lunches in many of the weekend menus, rather than sit-down meals with everyone together. All you have to do is set up the breakfast or sandwich bar and invite people to help themselves when they are hungry. At some point, someone will clean up and put the food away — and it needn't be you. Each menu is accompanied by a "Do Ahead" list and a "Weekend Work Plan." Here are some general plan-ahead ideas to help make any weekend entertaining run smoothly.

THINGS TO DO **BEFORE** THE WEEKEND ARRIVES

◆ Shop for staples the preceding weekend. Shop for meat and fresh produce mid-week. Pick up fresh bakery goods at the last minute.

◆ Do all the advance food preparation suggested in the selected menus.

◆ Prepare baked goods.

◆ Cut and chop veggies one day ahead and wrap each separately in plastic wrap.

◆ Wash and spin salad greens. Remove core from lettuce; separate leaves in a sink filled with cold water. Gently transfer greens to a large colander and let drain for a few minutes. Spin dry, wrap in a clean dish towel or paper towels. Store the leaves, towels and all, in a plastic bag in the refrigerator. Greens will keep fresh for several days this way.

◆ Organize your refrigerator.

◆ Check the suggested weekend work plan and adjust it as needed.

◆ Create a guest "work area," away from your own space. Plan specific tasks for guest helpers, depending on each one's competence in the kitchen. For example, put someone in charge of making the salad, give

WHAT CAN I BRING?

Whether you're a guest, or a host or hostess answering a guest's inquiry, here's our suggestion for the top ten items that will add to the weekend fun — counting down!

10 — Fresh bagels

9 — An appetizer, such as salsa

8 — Homemade or bakery bread with a special jam

7 — Homemade or bakery coffeecake

6 — Local specialty, like maple syrup from New England, wine from California, cheese from Wisconsin, jams from the Northwest, or chiles from the Southwest

5 — Selection of good pastas

4 — Specialty coffee beans

3 — Pantry specialty items: olive oils, flavored vinegars, and mustards

2 — A tin of homemade cookies

1 — *Weekend! A Menu Cookbook for Relaxed Entertaining*

another the dressing. If there's chopping to do, give a guest a cutting board and a knife and let them go to work. Don't forget to put the teenagers to work as well.

◆ Locate a buffet area for setting up a breakfast bar or "make-your-own" recipe ingredients. Plan another spot for drinks, and have plenty of ice available.

◆ Get thermoses for storing hot coffee — both decaf and regular.

◆ Have paper plates and napkins available.

◆ Identify the serving dishes you will need.

◆ For a big weekend, label your recycling containers so people know where to put recyclable bottles, cans, and so on.

◆ If little children are coming, stock up your pantry with food for them.

THINGS TO DO <u>DURING</u> THE WEEKEND

◆ Give assignments for setting up a sandwich bar.

◆ Put one person in charge of recycling and garbage, and have plenty of plastic and paper bags on hand.

◆ Give the non-cooks clean-up duty, and then stay out of the kitchen and let them do it.

◆ Make one person in charge of keeping the kids out of the kitchen during food preparation times.

◆ Have guests tidy up the kitchen and living areas before dinner.

◆ A half hour after everyone goes to bed, do a quick kitchen cleanup, set up the breakfast bar area for the morning, and fill the coffeepot.

◆ Tell guests what the morning routine is so they can help themselves and feel comfortable being autonomous.

◆ Put juice, coffee, and fruit out the night before for early rising guests.

◆ In the morning, finish setting up the basic breakfast bar, unless you plan a special breakfast.

◆ Early Sunday morning send someone out for several newspapers.

Above all, have a good time, and don't worry too much about the details.

BASIC BREAKFAST BAR SET-UP

On a counter or table with a toaster nearby, set up the following:

■ Plates, mugs, glasses, silver-ware, and napkins

■ Two kinds of juice

■ Decaf and regular coffee

■ Assorted teas, including decaf and herbal

■ Bakery breads (raisin and multigrain), English muffins, and several jams

■ Nonfat plain and vanilla yogurts

■ Low-fat cheeses

■ Granola

■ Cold cereals

■ Bananas and seasonal fruit

Take Good Care of Yourself — and Your Family and Friends

Entertaining and cooking for family and friends is one way of showing your concern for each other's well-being. Food is inextricably tied to health. Americans are deluged with information on hundreds of "diets" promising quick and easy cures for numerous health and weight problems. The number of conflicting claims is downright confusing. The truth is there are no quick and easy cures, but there is sound scientific advice recommending a varied diet low in sugar, total fat, and, particularly, saturated fat, while high in complex carbohydrates.

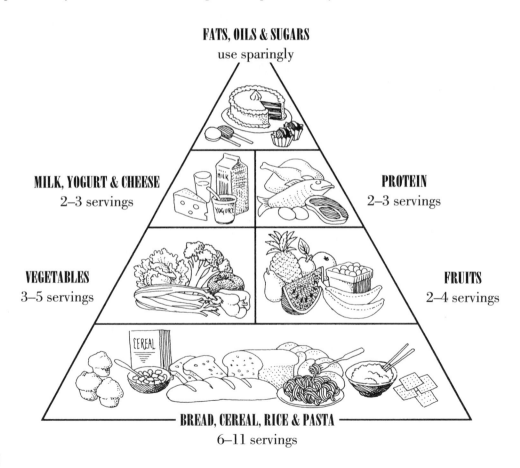

FATS, OILS & SUGARS
use sparingly

MILK, YOGURT & CHEESE
2–3 servings

PROTEIN
2–3 servings

VEGETABLES
3–5 servings

FRUITS
2–4 servings

BREAD, CEREAL, RICE & PASTA
6–11 servings

The Food Guide Pyramid developed by the United States Department of Agriculture reflects this advice. According to this source, most of our food should come from plants. In fact, of the recommended twenty-six servings of food daily for an adult male, 20 — or 77 percent — are grains, fruits, and vegetables. That is a *lot* of plant food to eat in one day — and if you substitute legumes for meat, it's even more! The guide also urges you to use sweets and fats sparingly.

About Fats

Fats are a highly concentrated form of energy, containing three times as many calories per gram as either carbohydrates or protein. This means that one tablespoon of oil contains 120 calories and 13.5 grams of fat. While we need some fat, the excess we consume is stored as fat tissue — in visible places (as we all know!). We need fat, but less is best, and unsaturated is preferable to saturated. For health reasons, knowing the difference between these two categories of fat is essential.

Saturated fats come from animals (meats and dairy products) and tropical oils (coconut and palm). Those from animals are solid at room temperature. Saturated fats raise cholesterol levels in the blood by increasing the amount of low-density lipoprotein (LDL) in the arteries, which is why we are advised to cut down on saturated fats to help prevent heart disease. We can reduce our intake by using skinless poultry and lean cuts of beef and pork, which are readily available as are low-fat or nonfat dairy products. Some low-fat cheeses taste great, others do not. Experiment until your taste buds are satisfied.

Unsaturated fats are liquid oils that come from vegetable sources and lower blood cholesterol. There are two varieties: monounsaturated (oils from olives, almonds, sesame seeds, canola, and avocados), and polyunsaturated (oils from walnuts, corn, sunflower, wheat germ, and soy), a distinction based on their chemical structure. The "polys" perform essential functions in the

A WORD ABOUT OLIVE OIL

Olive oil is one of the most important of the monounsaturated oils. Not only does this ancient oil, which has been used for centuries in both cooking and ritual, add a distinctive flavor to food, but it has been shown to lower blood cholesterol levels and decrease risk of coronary heart disease. Several studies of eating patterns in Mediterranean countries, where olive oil is the primary fat consumed, have confirmed a low rate of heart disease.

It is used as an essential flavoring in Mediterranean cooking and comes in many varieties from Italy, Greece, and Spain. In Tuscany, Italy, after the first olive oil is gently pressed in the early winter, people pour olive oil on everything and occasionally drink it.

While olive oil is a great flavoring, it is still a pure fat and should be used in moderation. Use good-quality oil, but don't be daunted by the huge selection available. For cooking, "non-virgin" oil, which is not from the first pressing, has most likely been heated, and may have some additives (including other types of oil), is fine. For flavoring, use oil labeled "extra-virgin" and preferably bottled on the premises where the olives are grown. This olive oil is cold pressed, has no additives, and will have the best flavor. It is also more expensive.

body, but in doing so release undesirable chemical by-products that pose health risks unless neutralized with antioxidant compounds such as vitamin E. "Monos," on the contrary, do not increase health risks and have been shown to lower cholesterol by increasing the amount of high-density lipoprotein (HDL), and keep it low. HDLs remove deposits from arterial walls, while also playing an important role in our body chemistry.

Hydrogenated Fats. To further complicate the issue, there are hydrogenated fats which are used in shortening, margarine, and creamy peanut butter. Liquid vegetable oil is transformed to a solid by introducing hydrogen which changes its chemical structure. In the process, some of the oil becomes saturated, and some becomes a trans-fatty acid. Unfortunately, these trans fats tend to *increase* LDL levels and decrease HDL levels; the result is increased cholesterol in the blood. So it is best to use these fats in small quantities even though they were originally unsaturated vegetable oils. In the butter versus margarine controversy we recommend butter, but in small quantities.

About Carbohydrates

Carbohydrates, complex starches and simple sugars that come from plants, are the main source of energy for our bodies. They supply important dietary fiber, as well as vitamins and minerals, and have little fat. We should try to increase the quantity of complex starches or whole grains in our diet and decrease the amount of simple sugars. Eating grain foods such as pasta, bread, rice, legumes, fruits, and vegetables is a great way to consume complex carbohydrates.

About Eating

We believe firmly that taste is the most important criteria in selecting recipes. We also believe in taking good care of ourselves, our families, and our friends by serving and eating healthy food. But eating healthy does *not* require sacrificing taste. Rather than completely giving up the old high-fat favorites, we alter them or eat less of them.

We have developed our recipes with flavor and health in mind. Some old favorites have been adjusted to maintain flavor while decreasing fats and

A WORD ABOUT FLOUR

Whole wheat pastry flour is used in many recipes in this book as a substitute for all-purpose flour. It is available in health food stores, but not always in supermarkets. It differs from whole wheat bread flour in that it is lighter, and lacks the gluten needed for the structure of bread. Because it is a delicate flour, it can readily be exchanged with white flour in all baked goods except bread, where the regular whole wheat flour is best. We have used whole wheat pastry flour frequently because it adds flavor, nutrition, and fiber. It is a perfect example of a complex carbohydrate.

increasing carbohydrates. Not every recipe fits the low-fat/high complex carbohydrate criteria, particularly for baked desserts, and here we urge restraint. Maintaining variety and balance in your diet is important over time, but it is not essential every day. If you overindulge one day, compensate for it the next day. But, know that it takes just a little high-fat food to qualify as overindulgence. We don't advocate obsessiveness, but we do hope that our menus will help you discover how great-tasting food can be made healthier.

Here are some tips for developing flavorful meals that are low in fat (particularly saturated fat) and high in complex carbohydrates.

◆ Select low-fat or nonfat dairy products, or use high-fat dairy products in small portions, substituting evaporated skimmed milk for cream and nonfat plain yogurt for sour cream (or use a mixture of the two). Evaporated skimmed milk can also be used for making whipped "cream" if both beaters and milk are icy cold.
◆ Choose fish and skinless poultry over red meat; use lean cuts of meat; prepare meat more as a garnish than the focus of a meal.
◆ Increase consumption of complex carbohydrate foods, including whole grains such as brown rice, oats, whole wheat, and rye, and fresh or lightly cooked fruits and vegetables.
◆ Use brown rice instead of white and substitute whole wheat pastry flour for some of the all-purpose flour called for in recipes.
◆ Flavor foods with herbs and spices.
◆ Restrict use of fats and oils by steaming vegetables rather than frying them, or sautéing in just 1 teaspoon instead of 1 to 2 tablespoons of oil.
◆ Spread only a thin layer of butter or other fat-rich toppings on bread or toast.
◆ Cut back on snacks and sweets filled with sugar, salt, and fat and substitute baked chips for fried.
◆ Substitute two egg whites for one whole egg, as we have done in many of our recipes.

The Cook's Pantry

A well-stocked cupboard, refrigerator, and freezer will help make your weekend entertaining — and all your cooking — run smoothly. Having a supply of ingredients on hand makes it easy to cook for guests and spontaneous events. Here's a list of the items we generally keep on hand, many of which are used in the recipes in this book.

IN THE CUPBOARD

Vegetable cooking spray
Chicken broth (canned)
Capers
Canned beans: cannellini, refried, and garbanzo
Dried beans (assorted kinds)
Plain tomato sauce (canned)
Italian chopped tomatoes (canned)
Tomato paste
Canola oil
Extra-virgin, good fruity olive oil for dressings and drizzling
Olive oil for cooking
Sun-dried tomatoes
Vinegars: flavored, red wine, white wine, balsamic, and cider
Salsa (bottled)
Green chiles (canned)
Crushed pineapple (canned and packed in juice)
Variety of herbs and spices (buy small quantities in bulk at a health food store)
Peppercorns (black and white)
Coarse salt
Unsweetened cocoa
Unsweetened baking chocolate
Wheat germ
Chocolate chips (although these have a tendency to disappear quickly!)
Brown sugar
Honey
Powdered skim milk
Evaporated skimmed milk (canned)

Mandarin oranges (canned)
Good (duram semolina) Italian pasta in a variety of shapes
Unbleached all-purpose flour
Baking soda and powder; cream of tartar
Garlic
Yellow onions
Red onions
Idaho baking potatoes
Red potatoes

IN THE FREEZER

Cranberries (not always available, so buy bags when they're in season and freeze)
Chopped onions (stored in a freezer bag)
Basil puree (When in season, chop bunches of basil in the food processor, add a little olive oil, and freeze in small containers for sauces and soups throughout the year.)
Grated low-fat mozzarella (grate a chunk and freeze in a bag)
Chopped cilantro (washed, dried, chopped, and stored in small freezer bags, for soups and fresh salsa all year)
Tomato chunks (When in season, wash, cut into 1-inch chunks, and store in freezer containers for fresh tomato sauce throughout the year — much easier than canning or making large batches of tomato sauce to freeze.)
Whole wheat pastry flour

Gingerroot (keeps well and can be grated while still frozen)
Almonds, walnuts, and pecans
Unsalted butter
Tortillas: corn, flour
Boneless, skinless chicken breasts

IN THE REFRIGERATOR

Nonfat plain yogurt
Lemons
Low-fat cottage cheese
Parmesan cheese
Low-fat cheddar cheese
Soft light margarine
Eggs
Skim milk
Orange juice
Mustard: Dijon, coarse, and sweet

FOR CHILDREN

Rice cakes: large and small (to decorate with peanut butter and raisin faces)
Clementines (small tangerines, easy to peel)
Brown paper lunch bags (kids can decorate and fill)
Applesauce, raisins, and string cheese in small containers
Makings for macaroni and cheese dinner
Fresh fruit
Tortillas (for sandwiches)
Apple juice in small containers

WINTER WEEKENDS

In New England, winter is a *real* season — cold and snowy — and a frequent topic of conversation. Whether you're one to stay inside by the fire and drink cocoa or to be outside skiing, you're sure to be talking and thinking about the weather. Winter has a mystique all its own. The first snowfall of the year excites young and old alike. While winter is the darkest season, there is something inspiring about the eerie blue light reflected off the snow on a starry or moonlit night.

Winter is a great time for cooking and sharing meals with friends. The urge to stay inside is strong. Curling up with a book, sipping tea by the fire, and eating hearty soups and stews are appealing pastimes. When the wind blows and the house feels a little cold, the smell of fresh bread baking, or a slow-cooking savory dish is sure to warm people up, on both the inside and the outside! Eating by candlelight has added meaning in winter as the flickering flame does indeed ward off the deep, dark night and create a cozy, snug atmosphere.

Cozy Winter Weekend by the Fire

Living in a cold wintery climate, you devise ways to enjoy the deep dark of winter. If it were possible to hibernate, I would, but the next best thing is to enjoy hearty, flavorful foods with people you care about. Snuggling by the fire sharing great food with good friends is one of the best ways I know to watch cold, dreary days go by. These are some of my favorite "stay-home-by-the-fire" foods. *E.S.*

~~~~~~~~~~

Saturday
Lunch
Soup au Pistou (French Vegetable Soup)*
Brioche or Egg Bread
Sliced Anjou Pears with Toasted Sliced Almonds

Supper
Jezz's Chili* • Brown Rice
Spinach Mushroom Salad with Creamy Lemon Vinaigrette*
Apple Sports Cake*

Sunday
Breakfast
Leftover Apple Cake
Poached Eggs with Tomato Hash on Toasted Egg Bread*
Orange and Grapefruit Juices

*recipe included

THINGS TO DO AHEAD

THE WEEKEND BEFORE
- Make and freeze Jezz's Chili
- Make and freeze Apple Sports Cake

MID-WEEK
- Shop for pears that are slightly hard; leave out so they are juicy and ripe for Saturday

FRIDAY EVENING
- Make Soup, except for the pistou, which is made at the last minute
- Thaw Chili and Apple Cake

SATURDAY MORNING
- Wash, spin, and store spinach
- Prepare Tomato Hash and refrigerate

WEEKEND WORK PLAN

SATURDAY MIDDAY
- Prepare Pistou for soup

SATURDAY EVENING
- Gently heat Chili
- Cook brown rice
- Prepare Spinach Mushroom Salad and Vinaigrette

SUNDAY MORNING
- Prepare Poached Eggs

Soup au Pistou (French Vegetable Soup)

Here is a simple version of this wonderful French Mediterranean soup. Pistou, the French version of pesto, turns a plain vegetable soup into a richly flavored, aromatic pleasure. My eighth-grade students love making and eating it.

Preparation Time: 1 hour • Serves 8

1½ quarts water
1 cup diced carrots
1 cup diced potatoes
1 cup diced onions
½ teaspoon salt
½ cup green beans
1 cup cooked navy or kidney beans
⅓ cup broken spaghetti
1 slice French bread
Freshly ground pepper, to taste
Pinch of saffron

Pistou

2 cloves garlic, mashed
2 tablespoons tomato paste
2 tablespoons finely chopped fresh basil, or 1 teaspoon dried
¼ cup grated Parmesan cheese
3 tablespoons olive oil

1. Combine the water, carrots, potatoes, and onions in a kettle; cook slowly for 30 minutes, or until the vegetables are tender. Season with salt. (This step can be done ahead of time.)

2. Add the green beans, navy beans, spaghetti, bread, and pepper; cook over medium heat for 15 minutes. Proceed to step 3, while soup cooks.

3. Make the pistou by whisking together the garlic, tomato paste, basil, and cheese in the bottom of a large casserole or soup tureen. Slowly beat in the olive oil. Beat 1 cup of the soup into the pistou. Then add the rest of the soup and mix well.

4. Serve immediately.

Jezz's Chili

I don't think of chili as a mainstay of English cooking, but Jezz, who is English, brought this delicious recipe with him when he moved to the States to marry my daughter Meg. It is not only a great meal, but it can also be put together quickly. Enlist the help of your guests with the cutting and chopping.

Preparation Time: 1 hour • Serves 6

1 pound lean ground beef
1 large onion, chopped
One 15-ounce can tomatoes with juice, chopped
3 tablespoons tomato paste
One 15-ounce can kidney beans, drained and rinsed
8 ounces fresh mushrooms, cut in half
1½–2 cups mixed red, yellow, and green peppers, cut into 1-inch chunks
2 beef bouillon cubes
1–2 tablespoons chili powder, or to taste
Dash of cayenne pepper (optional)
Salt and pepper, to taste

1. Sauté beef and onions in a large kettle over medium heat. Drain off half the fat with a bulb baster.

2. Add all the other ingredients to the pot; bring to a boil, turn heat down, and cover and simmer for 40 minutes.

Spinach Mushroom Salad with Creamy Lemon Vinaigrette

Preparation Time: 15 minutes • Serves 6

½ pound fresh spinach leaves, washed, trimmed, and dried
1 small head Boston or butter lettuce, washed and dried
1 cup sliced fresh mushrooms
1 Belgian endive, sliced
2 green onions, sliced

Vinaigrette
2 tablespoons fresh lemon juice
1 tablespoon white wine vinegar
1 clove garlic, minced
1 tablespoon Dijon mustard
¼–½ cup plain nonfat yogurt
1 tablespoon minced fresh parsley
Salt and freshly ground pepper, to taste

1. Toss the salad ingredients together in a large bowl.
2. Whisk the vinaigrette ingredients together and pour over the salad. Toss well and serve.

Apple Sports Cake

A wonderfully moist, flavorful cake that is appealing to the athletes in the crowd. When Kate's friends came to visit I offered this cake under another name to Chris, a runner, and Laura and Carrie. Chris declined, but when Carrie called it "Sports Cake," he gobbled up three pieces. It's been Sports Cake ever since!

Preparation Time: 30 minutes • Baking Time: 1 hour • Makes one 10-inch cake

1 large egg plus 2 egg whites
1 cup sugar
½ cup canola oil
½ cup apple butter
2 cups all-purpose flour
⅔ cup whole wheat pastry flour
3 tablespoons unsweetened cocoa
½ teaspoon salt
2 teaspoons baking soda
1 teaspoon ground cinnamon
1 teaspoon ground allspice
3 cups grated apples, peeled or unpeeled
1 cup raisins
½ cup chopped pecans
Confectioners' sugar (for dusting cake)

1. Preheat oven to 350°F.
2. Coat a 10-inch bundt pan with vegetable cooking spray; dust pan with flour and tap out excess.
3. In a large mixing bowl whisk together the eggs, sugar, oil, and apple butter. Sift the flours, cocoa, salt, soda, and spices together in a smaller bowl.
4. Add the dry ingredients to the egg mixture, alternating the flour mixture with the grated apples and stirring well after each addition. The batter will be very thick. Stir in the raisins and nuts. Spoon batter into the prepared pan.
5. Bake for 1 hour, or until a cake tester inserted in center comes out clean.
6. Cool cake on a wire rack for 10 minutes and remove from pan. Allow to cool completely, then dust with confectioners' sugar. Place on a pretty cake plate to serve.

Poached Eggs with Tomato Hash on Toasted Egg Bread

These are poached eggs with a flair, requiring a little extra effort, some of which can be done in advance! The result is so delicious that you'll be glad you did it.

Preparation Time: 30 minutes • Serves 6

1 egg plus 2 egg whites
¼ cup skim milk
Six 1-inch slices egg bread
1 teaspoon butter

Hash

4 ounces turkey breakfast sausage
2 tablespoons minced shallots
2 cups seeded and chopped fresh tomatoes
2 tablespoons finely chopped sun-dried tomatoes, packed in oil and drained
½ teaspoon rubbed sage
Salt and freshly ground pepper to taste

Eggs

¼ cup vinegar
6 eggs
3 tablespoons freshly grated Parmesan cheese

1. Whisk together the egg, egg whites, and milk. Dip slices of bread in egg mixture and set aside. Melt butter in a large nonstick skillet and pan toast the bread slices until they are all golden brown on both sides. Arrange on a foil-covered baking sheet and set aside.

2. Make the hash filling by cooking the sausage in the same skillet, breaking it up as finely as possible while it lightly browns. Remove from pan onto paper towels and wipe out pan.

3. Add shallots and fresh tomatoes to pan and cook for a few minutes. Next, add sun-dried tomatoes and cook a few more minutes. Finally, add sausage and seasonings and cook briefly. This can be done ahead and stored, covered, in the refrigerator.

4. Preheat broiler.

5. Prepare a large saucepan for cooking eggs by adding the vinegar to 4 inches of water; bring to a simmer. Crack each egg into a small dish and slip it into the simmering water. Poach for 2–4 minutes to desired doneness; remove with a slotted spoon and place on a paper towel to drain.

6. Spoon about 3 tablespoons tomato/sausage filling onto each piece of toast, leaving a small depression for the egg. Slip the eggs into the hot filling.

7. Sprinkle Parmesan cheese over the tops of the eggs. Broil 6 inches from heating element for 30 seconds and serve immediately.

Christmas with the Extended Family

A Time for Tradition

In the tradition of my German ancestry, Christmas Eve was the major holiday celebration and time of gift giving in my extended family. The meal inevitably featured herring salad and German cookies from Hoboken, creamed chicken on patty shells, and, always, my mother's cinnamon stars — all served on Aunt's most beautiful dishes. The memories and meals of our childhood often evolve into rituals for our own children as well. My children remember the creamed chicken at Aunt's, which has now become one of our own traditions.

As our family faced the difficulties of traveling and gathering an extended family together for Christmas, we developed a new tradition — sharing a candlelight Christmas Eve meal with a special family of close friends. The place, the people, the menu, and the dishes are different from earlier times, but the joy of the season remains. Another tradition we adopted years ago was to invite friends for a Christmas morning brunch after the presents were opened. Little kids were encouraged to bring their new toys and play while the grown-ups chatted and sipped wassail. Guests brought visiting parents and grandparents, making it seem like a large extended family. Today all the "little" kids are grown, and they bring their friends and spouses, and we all sip wassail. Certain foods have become traditional at this gathering which, for us, takes the place of a big Christmas dinner. *E.S.*

HOMEMADE FOOD TO GIVE AS GIFTS

Chocolate Hazelnut Biscotti*
Robin's Biscotti*
Herbed Vinegar
(in an unusual bottle)
Almond Butter Crunch*
Multibean soup mix
Cinnamon Stars*
Bittersweet Fudge Sauce*
(in a pretty jar,
see recipe on page 99)
Strawberry jam

*recipe included

Christmas Eve
Candlelight Dinner
Shrimp and Beef Fondue* with Assorted Sauces*
Special Onion Rice* • Crispy Green Salad
Multigrain Bread
Christmas Cookies and Ice Cream

Christmas Day
Early Breakfast for the Family Already Gathered
Grapefruit • Coffee and Cocoa
German Christmas Bread*
Scrambled Eggs

Brunch for Friends and Family
Jack's Christmas Wassail* • Hot Christmas Punch
Spinach Dip with Fresh Vegetables* • Pesto Torte (see recipe on page 82)
Little Dogs with Currant Mustard Sauce*
Roast Turkey Breast • Gravlax with Mustard Dill Sauce*
Cheese Board with Red and Green Seedless Grapes
Fruitcake* • German Christmas Bread* • Cinnamon Stars*
Hazelnut Coffee

recipe included

THINGS TO DO AHEAD

ONE WEEK BEFORE

- Make homemade gifts
- Make Cinnamon Stars and store in an airtight tin
- Make Fruitcake and wrap tightly in plastic wrap
- Get out needed dishes

FOUR DAYS BEFORE

- Make Christmas Bread and wrap tightly in plastic wrap
- Marinate Gravlax

THREE DAYS BEFORE

- Prepare Christmas Punch and store in refrigerator

TWO DAYS BEFORE

- Roast Turkey Breast
- Make sauces for Fondue and Mustard Dill Sauce for Gravlax

THE DAY BEFORE CHRISTMAS EVE

- Construct Pesto Torte; cover with plastic wrap and refrigerate
- Arrange cheese board; cover with plastic wrap and refrigerate
- Prepare Spinach Dip; mound in serving bowl, cover with plastic wrap, and refrigerate
- Wash, spin, and store salad greens

WEEKEND WORK PLAN

CHRISTMAS EVE DAY

- Clean shrimp and cut up beef for Fondue
- Prepare Special Onion Rice
- Set a beautiful table
- Prepare green salad

CHRISTMAS MORNING

- Have someone set table for breakfast
- Clear table and prepare it for brunch
- Assign someone to make wassail and punch
- Assign someone to cut up vegetables
- Slice Turkey and Gravlax
- Prepare Little Dogs with Currant Mustard Sauce
- Arrange dip and vegetables
- Set food out on the table

SPECIALTY ITEMS NEEDED

- Fondue pot
- Long-handled forks

Shrimp and Beef Fondue

Eight people is a good number for one fondue pot. This recipe makes for a congenial, interactive meal. Give each person two long fondue forks so they can cook either beef or shrimp until sated. At least three different sauces provide a nice variety of flavors for dipping. Try salsa, Mustard Sauce (see recipe on page 77), Curry Sauce (use Mustard Sauce recipe, substituting curry powder for Dijon mustard), Horseradish Sauce, or Spinach Dressing.

Preparation Time: 30 minutes • Serves 8

1 quart peanut oil
1½–2 pounds boneless beef tenderloin, sirloin, or filet of
   beef, cut into 1-inch cubes
1½ pounds, fresh shrimp (large or jumbo), shelled

1. At the table pour peanut oil into a fondue pot with sides that curve inward to avoid spattering. Heat to temperature at which a piece of shrimp dropped in cooks quickly.
2. Arrange the raw beef on one platter and the raw shrimp on another; pass around the table. Serve the sauces in small bowls.
3. When the oil is hot, have each person spear the food of choice and cook it in the hot oil; eat with one of the sauces. A leisurely meal pace is recommended to avoid competitive cooking.

Horseradish Sauce

½ cup light sour cream
¼ cup plain nonfat yogurt
2 tablespoons mayonnaise
2 tablespoons horseradish

Combine all ingredients and mix well.

Spinach Dressing

2 cups tender spinach leaves
3 tablespoons lemon juice
Salt and freshly ground black pepper, to taste
¼ cup olive oil

1. In a food processor combine the spinach leaves, lemon juice, salt, and pepper until well blended.
2. Slowly add the olive oil and process until the sauce is blended and slightly thickened.

Special Onion Rice

Our friend Sandy makes this wonderfully tasty rice and serves it with the fondue on Christmas eve. We love it! It also has a nice, make-it-in-advance quality.

Don't be surprised by the unconventional cooking method. The large quantity of onions supplies all the liquid necessary to puff the grains. I can usually get through five onions before I'm blinded by tears. Over the years students have given me many tips to avoid this plight, and my favorite is to slice onions with a piece of bread in your mouth. Usually I just slice away and have a good cry.

Preparation Time: 30 minutes • Baking Time: 1 hour • Serves 10

2 tablespoons butter
2 pounds onions (about 6 large onions), sliced
4 quarts water with ½ teaspoon salt added
2 cups short grain brown rice
½ teaspoon salt
¼ teaspoon freshly ground pepper
¼ cup half-and-half or evaporated skimmed milk, warmed
1 cup grated good-quality Swiss cheese

1. Preheat oven to 300°F.
2. Melt the butter in a large ovenproof, flameproof casserole. Stir in the onions and cook over low heat until they are completely coated with the butter.
3. In a large pot, bring the salted water to a rapid boil; add the rice and boil for 5 minutes to soften the grain. Drain the rice, add it to the onions along with salt and pepper, and stir until well blended. Cover and bake for 1 hour.
4. Remove from oven, cool slightly, and refrigerate.
5. Before serving, add about ½ cup water and reheat rice over low heat. When hot, add warmed half-and-half and cheese. Stir and serve.

Christmas Wassail

The drink we love to hate! Jack makes several batches of this potent punch every Christmas morning and serves it at our annual brunch. On any other day we wouldn't touch it, but on Christmas, with all the warm and wonderful smells and tastes, it is perfect! The custom of drinking a toast makes sense after partaking of this wassail. If one is lucky, one can *literally* drink a toast because it is floating in the hot spiced ale along with the roasted apples. The drink itself dates back to Medieval England where the name wassail meant "Be hale."

Preparation Time: 45 minutes • Makes 1½ quarts, about 12 servings

7 crab apples or 3 small Macintosh apples, washed and
　pricked with the tines of a fork
1 quart ale
1 teaspoon freshly grated nutmeg
5 slices gingerroot
2 cups sherry wine
Juice and the thinly pared rind of 1 lemon
2 tablespoons sugar
3 pieces of bread, toasted and cut into quarters

1. Preheat oven to 450°F.
2. Roast apples for 10–25 minutes depending on their size, until they are just soft. Set aside and keep warm.
3. Heat ale in a large enameled or stainless steel kettle over medium heat until just below the boiling point. Stir in spices, sherry, lemon juice and rind, and sugar. Cover and steep over low heat for 25 minutes. Do not boil.
4. Strain the wassail into a heated punch bowl and float apples and toast on top.
5. Ladle hot wassail into punch cups and drink a toast.

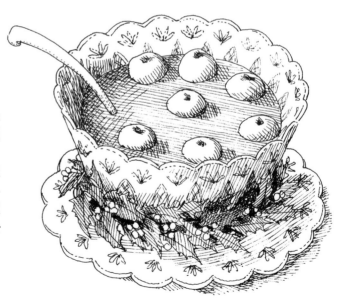

Spinach Dip

This healthy, delicious, familiar dip can be easily doubled to feed a crowd.

Preparation Time: 20 minutes • Chilling Time: 2 hours • Makes 2 cups

One 10-ounce package frozen chopped spinach, thawed
   and squeezed dry
¼ cup well-mixed dry vegetable soup mix
½ cup plain nonfat yogurt
3 tablespoons light mayonnaise
½ cup mock sour cream
½ cup water chestnuts, drained and chopped
½ cup chopped chives or green onions

   In a medium-size bowl combine all the ingredients
and mix well. Chill and serve with raw vegetables.

Mock Sour Cream
Makes 1 cup

1 cup low-fat cottage cheese
2 tablespoons buttermilk
½–1 teaspoon freshly squeezed lemon juice

   Combine all the ingredients in a blender and blend
until smooth, scraping the sides of the container often
with a rubber spatula.

Little Dogs with Currant Mustard Sauce

These dogs are definitely *not* in the low-fat category, but we always have them. They disappear quickly, couldn't
be simpler to make, and just taste great!

Preparation Time: 20 minutes • Serves 8–12 as appetizers

1 pound miniature *kielbasa* (Polish smoked sausage) or
   little hot dogs, or a combination
2 tablespoons Dijon mustard
½ cup currant jelly

1.   Preheat oven to 350°F.
2.   Roast sausages for 15 minutes, or until they are
slightly browned.

3.   Mix the mustard and jelly in a chafing dish; heat in
the oven until the jelly melts and the mixture is
smooth. Add the sausages and keep warm. Serve in
a chafing dish with toothpicks, more mustard, and/
or horseradish.

Gravlax with Mustard Dill Sauce

In the process of teaching about Swedish cooking, I once served gravlax at a neighborhood dinner party with a Swedish theme. My next gravlax experience was in Stockholm, when our Swedish friend Binge served it to us with special Swedish mustard. We loved it! It is about to become a regular on our Christmas brunch table. Gravlax is really quite simple to make and a wonderful addition to the salmon lover's repertoire. The secret, of course, is getting very fresh salmon.

Preparation Time: 15 minutes • Marinating Time: Several days • Serves 8–10

3 pounds fresh salmon fillets, cut, cleaned, scaled, and cut in half lengthwise
One large bunch of fresh dill
¼ cup coarse salt
¼ cup sugar
Crushed white or black peppercorns

1. Rinse the fillets and pat dry; lay half the fillet pieces skin side down in a glass or enameled baking pan. Spread a layer of dill over the salmon and sprinkle with salt, sugar, and pepper. Top with the other half of the salmon and cover lightly with plastic wrap.

2. Place a cutting board on the salmon and load heavy objects on the board. (This is a good use for barbells you may have hanging around the house!) Marinate the salmon for 2–3 days in the refrigerator, turning several times. The salmon will compact slightly from the weights.

3. When ready to serve, scrape off the marinade and thinly slice the gravlax on the diagonal. Serve with Swedish mustard or mustard dill sauce on thin rye crackers or rye bread.

Mustard Dill Sauce

Preparation Time: 10 minutes • Makes ¾ cup

4 tablespoons dark, spicy mustard
1 teaspoon dry mustard
3 tablespoons sugar
3 tablespoons white vinegar
¼ cup canola oil
3 tablespoon chopped fresh dill

In a small bowl whisk together the mustards, sugar, and vinegar. Slowly drizzle in the oil, whisking all the time until the sauce is thick. Stir in the dill and serve.

Fruitcake

This is the best fruitcake I have ever eaten. If you are one of the special breed who likes fruitcake, try this one. It is complex, moist, delicious, and, of course, keeps forever — well, at least six months in the refrigerator. It's a bit of a production to make fruitcake because of all the ingredients, but the method is quite simple.

Preparation Time: 30 minutes • Baking Time: 2–3 hours • Makes 1 large loaf

1 cup candied pineapple, diced (I buy honeyed pineapple at the health food store)
½ cup candied cherries, halved
3 tablespoons chopped candied citron
3 tablespoons chopped candied lemon peel
3 tablespoons chopped candied orange peel
1⅓ cups golden raisins
⅔ cup dark raisins
½ cup currants
⅔ cup unblanched almonds, coarsely chopped
1 cup walnuts, coarsely chopped
1½ cups all-purpose flour
¼ teaspoon allspice
¼ teaspoon cinnamon
¼ teaspoon baking soda
3 eggs
3 tablespoons brandy
3 tablespoons applesauce
½ teaspoon almond extract
¼ cup unsalted butter, softened
½ cup sugar
½ cup brown sugar

1. Preheat oven to 275°F. Lightly grease a 9 by 5 by 3-inch loaf pan, or two 1-pound coffee cans; line bottom and sides with oiled brown paper and grease again.

2. In a large bowl combine the pineapple, cherries, citron, lemon and orange peels, light and dark raisins, currants, almonds, walnuts, and ½ cup of the flour. Toss well to mix and set aside.

3. Sift the rest of the flour with the allspice, cinnamon, and baking soda; set aside.

4. In a small bowl beat the eggs until they are light. Beat in the brandy, applesauce, and almond extract and set aside.

5. In the large bowl of an electric mixer, beat butter and sugars at medium speed until light and fluffy. Gradually add the egg mixture. At low speed, gradually beat in the flour, beating only until combined.

6. Add the fruit and nut mixture to the batter and stir with a large spatula or wooden spoon until well mixed. Pour the batter into the pan; smooth the top and bake for 3 hours for a large single cake, 2 hours for two coffee-can cakes, or until a cake tester comes out clean. Cool in pan for 30 minutes on a wire rack.

7. Remove cake from pan and cool completely on a wire rack. Wrap cakes tightly in plastic wrap and store in the refrigerator until ready to serve or give as gifts.

German Christmas Bread

Sweet bread was not part of my German family's Christmas table, but a number of years ago I started making this incredibly good quick bread. I make three or four batches each season. It keeps well and makes lovely gifts.

Preparation Time: 30 minutes • Baking Time: 45 minutes • Makes 1 loaf

2½ cups all-purpose flour
2 teaspoons baking powder
¾ cup sugar
½ teaspoon salt
½ teaspoon mace
⅛ teaspoon ground cardamom
¾ cup ground almonds
½ cup cold unsalted butter
1 cup low-fat cottage cheese, forced through a sieve
1 egg, slightly beaten
½ teaspoon vanilla
¼ teaspoon almond extract
2 tablespoons rum, or ½ teaspoon rum extract mixed
  with 2½ tablespoons water
½ cup currants
½ cup golden raisins
¼ cup candied lemon peel
1 tablespoon melted butter
2 tablespoons vanilla sugar
  (made by burying a vanilla bean in 1 cup sugar for
  2–3 days to perfume the sugar)

1. Preheat oven to 350°F. Cover an ungreased baking sheet with brown paper or parchment paper.

2. In a large bowl combine the flour, baking powder, sugar, salt, mace, cardamom, and almonds. With a pastry blender cut in the butter until the mixture resembles coarse crumbs.

3. In another large bowl blend the cottage cheese, egg, vanilla, almond extract, rum, currants, raisins, and lemon peel. Stir in the flour mixture until all the ingredients are moistened. Mold the dough into a ball and knead on a floured surface about ten times. The dough will be soft and bumpy.

4. Shape or roll the dough to form an 8½ by 10-inch oval. Lightly crease the dough with the handle of the rolling pin, slightly off center, and parallel to the long side. Brush the dough lightly with melted butter, and fold the smaller side over the larger side to form an irregular oval loaf.

5. Bake on the prepared baking sheet for 45 minutes, or until the crust is browned and a toothpick inserted in the center comes out clean.

6. Brush the loaf with the remaining butter and sprinkle with the vanilla sugar. Cool completely on a wire rack. Wrap in plastic wrap and store for several days to ripen the flavors.

Chocolate Hazelnut Biscotti

Biscotti — hard, sweet biscuits — are as varied as the regions of Italy where they originated. The chocolate and hazelnuts add a festive touch to this version of the twice-cooked Italian speciality.

Preparation Time: 30 minutes • Baking Time: 30 minutes • Finishing Time: 15 minutes • Makes 4 dozen

1 cup hazelnuts (also called filberts)
½ cup butter, softened
¾ cup sugar
1 tablespoon grated orange peel
3 eggs
1 teaspoon vanilla
3 cups flour
1 tablespoon baking powder
½ teaspoon salt
1 cup (one 6-ounce package) semisweet chocolate baking chips

1. Preheat oven to 350°F.
2. Place the hazelnuts in an 8-inch square baking pan and bake for 18–20 minutes or until lightly toasted, shaking the pan occasionally. Remove from oven, leaving oven on. Pour the nuts onto a clean kitchen towel and when cool, rub them with the cloth to remove most of the skins. Lift out the nuts, chop coarsely, and set them aside.
3. In a large bowl cream the butter, sugar, and orange peel until light and fluffy. Add the eggs, one at a time, beating well after each addition. Stir in the vanilla.
4. Combine the flour, baking powder, and salt; add to the butter mixture. Stir to blend thoroughly. Mix in the hazelnuts.
5. Divide the dough into thirds. Shape each third into a long roll, about 1½ inches in diameter. Place the rolls 2 inches apart on a sprayed 12 by 15-inch baking sheet. Flatten the rolls to a ½-inch thickness. Bake for 15 minutes.
6. Remove rolls from the oven and cut crosswise into ¾-inch thick slices. Lay cut side down on a greased baking sheet. Return to the oven and continue baking for about 15 minutes, until the biscotti look dry and are lightly browned. Remove them from baking sheets and cool on wire racks.
7. In a small saucepan stir the chocolate over very low heat until it is just melted. Spread chocolate on the top and sides of one end of each biscotti. When chocolate is firm, serve or store in an airtight container for up to two days. Freeze to store longer.

Robin's Biscotti

Robin is a wonderful chef whose creations have delighted diners in many restaurants in the Berkshire hills of Massachusetts. She recently opened Robin's Restaurant and agreed to share her popular biscotti recipe.

Preparation Time: 30 minutes • Baking Time: 50 minutes • Drying Time: 1½ hours • Makes 4 dozen

6 ounces grated almonds
2½ cups flour
1 cup sugar
1 teaspoon salt
1 teaspoon baking soda
¼ cup butter, very soft
3 eggs or 6 egg whites, slightly beaten
1½ teaspoon vanilla, or other flavoring such as anisette
¼ cup plus 1 tablespoon water
6 ounces chopped almonds, toasted at 350°F for 6 minutes

1. Preheat oven to 375°F.
2. In a large bowl combine the grated almonds, flour, sugar, salt, and baking soda.
3. In a small bowl mix the butter, eggs or egg whites, flavoring, and water. Pour the liquid ingredients into the flour mixture all at once. Mix into a sticky dough. Add the toasted chopped almonds. The dough will be very sticky.
4. Thoroughly flour your hands and the work surface on which you will shape loaves and work quickly (as the heat from your hands makes the dough stickier). Form the dough into 2 loaves, each about 4 inches wide, 1½ inches high, and 10–12 inches long. Place loaves on a sprayed and floured baking sheet. Bake for 50 minutes, or until golden brown.
5. Remove loaves from pan and slice with a serrated knife into ½-inch thick slices. Place slices flat side down on baking sheet and dry in a 200°F oven for about 1½ hours. Turn them once after 45 minutes. Remove from oven and store in airtight containers.

Almond Butter Crunch

Fortunately we only get butter crunch once a year when Sandy and Bev present us with packages of these delectable sweets. I show absolutely no control when it's around.

Preparation Time: 1 hour • Makes enough to share with 4–6 friends

1 cup butter
1⅓ cups granulated sugar
1 tablespoon light corn syrup
3 tablespoons water
1 cup *coarsely* chopped, toasted, blanched almonds
Four 4½-ounce bars milk chocolate, melted
1 cup *finely* chopped blanched almonds, toasted

1. Melt the butter in a heavy 2-quart saucepan. Add the sugar, corn syrup, and water; cook, stirring frequently until the syrup reaches the hard crack stage, 300°F on a candy thermometer. Quickly stir in the coarsely chopped almonds.

2. Spread the mixture in a well-greased 13 by 9 by 2-inch pan or on a greased marble slab and let cool.

3. Turn the cooled candy out onto a sheet of wax paper. Spread the surface with half of the melted chocolate and sprinkle with half of the finely chopped almonds. Cover with wax paper and invert; spread the toppings on the other side. Chill the candy until it is firm, then break into pieces. Store in airtight container.

Cinnamon Stars

This traditional chewy cookie, made with egg whites and ground almonds and iced with a cinnamon meringue, comes from Germany and is almost always on our Christmas table.

Preparation Time: 1–1½ hours • Makes 4 dozen

1 pound finely ground unblanched almonds
¼ teaspoon salt
1 teaspoon grated lemon rind
5 egg whites, at room temperature
2 cups sifted confectioners' sugar
2 teaspoons ground cinnamon

1. Preheat oven to 325°F. Coat baking sheets with vegetable cooking spray.
2. In a large bowl mix the almonds, salt, and lemon rind.
3. In the large bowl of an electric mixer beat the egg whites until soft peaks form. Continue beating and slowly add the sugar, a small amount at a time, until stiff peaks form. Stir in the cinnamon.
4. Take about a quarter of the egg white mixture and add to almonds. Stir until well mixed. The dough tends to be sticky and very fragile. (Save the rest of the meringue for Step 6, below.)
5. On a wooden board dusted with confectioners' sugar, roll out a small amount of dough until ⅛-inch thick and use a star-shaped cutter to cut out cookies. Use additional confectioners' sugar when the dough sticks. It's a messy job but well worth the effort.
6. Ice each cookie with a small amount of the remaining egg white meringue. Bake cookies for 20 minutes or until slightly browned. Remove from baking sheets immediately and cool on racks. Store in an airtight container. They keep for several weeks.

New Year's Celebration

New Year's Eve and Day are the last festive gasps before the onset of new diets, budgets, and exercise plans that punctuate the start of a new year. With my daughters, Wendy and Liza, I have been debating about the food for this memorable evening. Wendy feels that it should be truly spectacular, while Liza and I feel we have had enough of spectacular by New Year's Eve and want to slow down to something a bit simpler. The following menu pleases us all.

We often celebrate quietly with a few close friends, sometimes writing out resolutions to be opened the following year. There are usually small favors for each guest, twinkling bow ties or perhaps small plastic kazoos. Since the evening starts and ends late, it is nice to have guests spend the night. Breakfast the next morning is minimal. Sleepy celebrants are recruited to help chop and assemble the Hoppin' John. *P.W.*

~~~~~~~~~~~~~~~~

New Year's Eve
Buffet
Spinach Salad with Poppy Seed Dressing*
(see recipe on page 36)
Sliced Beef Tenderloin* • Shrimp and Feta Casserole*
Crusty Seven Grain Rolls
White Angel Cake • Chocolate Angel Cake* with
Raspberry Puree* or Mocha Glop*

Note: Although we have included a recipe for the chocolate angel cake, we decided that the store-bought mixes for white angel cakes are as good as what we could come up with and a great deal easier.

New Year's Day
Morning
Grapefruit Halves
English Muffins with Orange Marmalade
Kona Blend Coffee

Afternoon
Tana's Hoppin' John with Smoked Turkey*
Brown Rice
Orange and Avocado Slices with Cumin Vinaigrette*
(see recipe on page 36)
Cornbread Squares

*recipe included

THINGS TO DO AHEAD

THE WEEKEND BEFORE

■ Prepare Poppy Seed Dressing and
  Cumin Vinaigrette

THE DAY BEFORE

■ Bake Angel Cakes
■ Wash, spin, and store spinach for salad
■ Prepare Tana's Hoppin' John with Smoked Turkey

SPECIALTY ITEMS NEEDED

■ Smoked turkey breast

WEEKEND WORK PLAN

NEW YEAR'S EVE MORNING

■ Prepare Shrimp and Feta Casserole
■ Prepare Raspberry Puree

NEW YEAR'S EVE MIDDAY

■ Roast the Beef Tenderloin
■ Prepare Mocha Glop

NEW YEAR'S EVE

■ Bake Shrimp and Feta Casserole
■ Slice the Beef Tenderloin
■ Prepare salad
■ Warm rolls

NEW YEAR'S DAY MORNING

■ Arrange breakfast foods for self-service

NEW YEAR'S DAY MIDDAY

■ Cook brown rice
■ Warm Tana's Hoppin' John
■ Chop red onion for Tana's Hoppin' John
■ Prepare orange and avocado salad

Sliced Beef Tenderloin

Preparation Time: 15 minutes • Cooking Time: About 45 minutes for rare, longer for well-done • Serves 8

1 beef tenderloin, trimmed (about 4 pounds after trimming)
2 tablespoons coarsely ground white peppercorns
Parchment paper

1. Preheat oven to 425°F.
2. Line the bottom of a 9 by 13-inch glass baking dish with parchment paper. Sprinkle with 1 tablespoon of the ground pepper. Tuck tail under meat and place in pan on parchment paper. Press remaining peppercorns into top surface of meat. Insert meat thermometer into thickest part of meat.
3. Roast meat in center of hot oven until thermometer registers 130°F (about 45 minutes). Wrap whole and refrigerate.
4. Fifteen minutes before serving carve into ½-inch slices.

Shrimp and Feta Casserole

This unique combination is one of my personal favorites.

Preparation Time: 30 minutes • Baking Time: 30 minutes • Serves 8

8 ounces feta cheese
2 large eggs
1 cup evaporated skimmed milk
1 cup low-fat yogurt
6 ounces Swiss cheese, shredded
⅓ cup fresh chopped parsley
1 tablespoon finely chopped fresh basil, or 1 teaspoon dried
1 tablespoon finely chopped fresh oregano, or 1 teaspoon dried
3 cloves garlic, minced
8 ounces angel-hair pasta, cooked
One 16-ounce jar mild salsa
1 pound medium shrimp, raw and peeled
8 ounces part-skim mozzarella, shredded

1. Preheat oven to 350°F.
2. Coat the bottom and sides of an 8 by 12-inch casserole with vegetable cooking spray.
3. Quickly rinse feta cheese in cold water; pat dry and crumble.
4. In a medium-size bowl thoroughly blend eggs, milk, yogurt, feta cheese, Swiss cheese, parsley, basil, oregano, and garlic.
5. Spread half of the pasta over the bottom of the casserole. Cover with the salsa; add half of the shrimp; cover with the remaining pasta.
6. Pour egg mixture evenly over pasta. Add remaining shrimp and sprinkle mozzarella over top.
7. Bake for 30 minutes. Let casserole stand for 15 minutes before serving.

Chocolate Angel Cake

Dutching is a process that neutralizes the acidity in cocoa powder and produces a powder both darker and more mellow than traditional cocoa. You'll find using it for this recipe results in a cake light enough to avoid guilt yet rich enough to delight your chocolate lovers.

Preparation Time: 30 minutes • Baking Time: 35 minutes • Makes one 10-inch cake

¾ cup cake flour
¼ cup Dutch process cocoa
1¼ cups sugar
10 large egg whites (at room temperature)
¼ teaspoon salt
1 teaspoon cream of tartar
½ teaspoon vanilla

1. Place baking rack in the center of the oven. Preheat oven to 350°F.
2. Sift together flour and cocoa until well blended. Add ¼ cup sugar and sift again into a large bowl; set aside.
3. In a clean bowl gently beat the egg whites with salt. Add cream of tartar and increase beater speed. Beat until soft peaks are formed when beater is raised. Gradually beat in remaining sugar, a tablespoon at a time until stiff peaks form. Blend in vanilla.
4. Sift a little of the flour mixture over the egg whites and fold it in with a large spatula. Repeat this process until all the flour is used. Do not fold mixture more than is necessary as too much mixing will keep the cake from rising.
5. Gently transfer mixture to an ungreased 10-inch tube pan. Bake for 35 minutes without opening the oven door. After 35 minutes test with a toothpick; it should come out clean and cake center should come back when pressed lightly.
6. When done, invert the cake and suspend the pan by placing the opening in the center of the tube pan over the neck of a wine bottle. Allow to cool for at least 1½ hours. Loosen the cake from the sides of the pan very carefully with a sharp knife.

Note: To serve, gently pull the cake apart with two forks or carefully slice with a bread knife. Top with Raspberry Puree, Mocha Glop, or both (see following recipes).

Raspberry Puree

Preparation Time: 10 minutes • Makes 2 cups

One 10-ounce package frozen, unsweetened raspberries
1 teaspoon Kirsch

Puree raspberries in a blender or food processor. If the seeds bother you, press the mixture through a sieve. Stir in Kirsch. Chill until ready to serve.

Mocha Glop

The combination of angel cake and this simple topping was a staple of my parents' dinner parties. I have tried to make this old favorite just a bit healthier.

Preparation Time: 15 minutes • Serves 8

1 cup heavy cream
¼ cup confectioners' sugar, sifted
¼ cup unsweetened cocoa powder
½ cup low-fat yogurt

1. Chill mixing bowl and beaters in freezer.
2. In the chilled bowl mix together the cream, sugar, and cocoa powder. Beat with chilled beaters until stiff enough to hold a peak; blend in yogurt and chill thoroughly. Pile in a pretty glass serving bowl and allow guests to top their angel cake with a dollop.

Note: To cut out the fat, try beating 1½ cups icy cold evaporated skimmed milk in place of the cream and adding all the other ingredients except the yogurt.

Poppy Seed Dressing

Preparation Time: 10 minutes • Makes 1½ cups (Use about ½ cup for a pound of clean prepared spinach leaves)

1 cup canola oil
½ cup cranberry juice
1 teaspoon salt
¼ cup honey
1 tablespoon dried mustard
1 tablespoon grated onion
1½ tablespoons poppy seeds

Combine oil, juice, salt, honey, mustard, and onion in a glass jar; shake until honey is well blended with other ingredients. Add poppy seeds and shake well.

Note: This dressing can be stored in the refrigerator for several weeks. Bring it to room temperature and shake it when ready to use. Toss it with clean, chilled, tender fresh spinach leaves.

Cumin Vinaigrette

Preparation Time: 15 minutes • Makes about ½ cup

5 tablespoons extra-virgin olive oil
1 tablespoon red wine vinegar
1 tablespoon orange juice
1 teaspoon sugar
4 teaspoons ground cumin
1 small clove garlic, minced

Whisk together all the ingredients. Cover and let stand for at least 1 hour, or up to 2 days in the refrigerator.

Tana's Hoppin' John with Smoked Turkey

Our friend Tana developed this healthy version of the traditional New Year's Day good-luck dish without losing a bit of flavor.

Preparation Time: About 5 hours start to finish, but only about 40 minutes of concentrated attention • Serves 6–8

1 pound black-eyed peas
1½ pounds hot turkey sausage links
¼ pound smoked turkey breast, cut in ½-inch cubes (available at most delicatessen counters; ask for a chunk, not slices)
6 cups chicken broth
1 tablespoon olive oil
1 tablespoon crushed garlic
1 onion, finely chopped
1 cup finely chopped celery
2 bay leaves
2 teaspoons crushed red pepper
1 teaspoon dried thyme
1 tablespoon dried basil
Chopped red onion
Tabasco sauce

1. Cover peas with water and bring to a boil; boil for 2 minutes. Remove from heat, cover pot, and let stand for 1 hour; drain.

2. Slice turkey sausage into ½-inch pieces and brown in a heavy kettle. Add black-eyed peas, smoked turkey, and broth to sausage and bring to a boil.

3. In a saucepan heat the oil; sauté garlic, onion, and celery and add to the turkey/pea mixture. Add bay leaves and other seasoning. Simmer covered for 2 hours.

4. Uncover and simmer for 15 to 20 minutes, or until peas are just tender and liquid is thickened. Do not overcook or it will become mushy. Ladle into an earthenware crock and serve with red onion and tabasco sauce as toppings.

A Weekend in Ski Country

Snowfall is not only welcomed in ski country — it is *longed* for. Those who seek the thrill of maneuvering down a steep slope, or enjoy the tranquility of gliding through silent woods in crisp, clear air know the joys of snow skiing.

When you become tired of hunkering down and staying cozy in winter, it's time to get outside and do something active, like spending a weekend skiing with friends, especially when the sun is shining. Or, even if it isn't: A Norwegian friend who lives above the Arctic Circle speaks of beautiful light that reflects off the snow on those long, dark winter days when the sun doesn't rise. They ski every Sunday. These hearty meals are designed to fuel your outdoor activities. *E.S.*

Friday
Arrival Supper

Five Cheese Spaghetti* • Chunky Tomato Mushroom Sauce*
Sautéed Broccoli and Garlic*
Focaccia with Sage and Rosemary*
Fresh Fruit

Saturday
Breakfast

Hot Oatmeal with Brown Sugar
Stewed Oranges and Apricots* • Assorted Juices
Hot Homemade Cocoa*
Coffee/Tea

Have lunch on the slopes

Aprés Ski

*(served as people dribble in from the slopes or
cross-country trails)*
Aprés Ski Snacks* • Hot Cider

Late Supper

Stifado*
Crusty Sesame Seed Bread • Crispy Green Salad
Baked Alaska*

Sunday
Breakfast for a Second Day of Skiing

Scrambled Eggs
Toasted Multigrain Bread with Apple Butter
Assorted Juices • Coffee/Tea/Cocoa

*recipe included

THINGS TO DO AHEAD

THE WEEKEND BEFORE

- Grate cheeses for Spaghetti and store in heavy zip-seal bags in freezer
- Prepare Focaccia dough and store in freezer
- Bake cake for Alaska and freeze
- Prepare Stewed Oranges and Apricots

WEDNESDAY

- Assemble Baked Alaska
- Prepare topping for Aprés Ski Snacks

THURSDAY

- Prepare Stifado and refrigerate
- Steam Broccoli and store in a zip-seal bag in refrigerator

FRIDAY MORNING

- Thaw cheeses and Focaccia dough in refrigerator

SPECIALTY ITEMS NEEDED

- One 10 to 12-inch cardboard cake round (available in bakeries)

WEEKEND WORK PLAN

FRIDAY EVENING

- Roll out Focaccia dough; finish preparing and bake
- Cook spaghetti and make sauce
- Sauté garlic and gently heat Broccoli

SATURDAY MORNING

- Set up breakfast area
- Prepare Hot Oatmeal
- Warm Stewed Fruit
- Make Cocoa
- Go ski and have fun!

SATURDAY EVENING

- Warm Stifado
- Heat bread
- Prepare salad (a good job for a helper)
- Remove Baked Alaska from freezer when you sit down to eat
- Put Alaska in oven just before serving

SUNDAY MORNING

- Assemble a coffee and juice area
- Prepare cocoa
- Have someone toast bread
- Cook eggs
- Go off to the slopes or the trails for another great day of skiing!

Five Cheese Spaghetti

This is by no means a low-fat pasta dish — but you should have seen it *before* we altered it to cut the fat as much as we could. The wonderfully rich flavor obtained by combining these cheeses is still there, and it is worth every gram of fat that remains. An alternative to the cheese sauce is the light Chunky Tomato Mushroom Sauce.

Preparation Time: 20 minutes • Serves 6

2 cups skim milk
2 tablespoons cornstarch
1 teaspoon unsalted butter
½ cup grated Edam cheese
½ cup grated provolone cheese
½ cup grated Gruyère cheese
½ cup grated Italian Fontina cheese
1–1½ pound spaghetti (a thick vermicelli)
1 tablespoon olive oil
¼ cup freshly grated Parmesan cheese for topping

1. Combine the milk and cornstarch in large, heavy saucepan. Bring to a boil to thicken, lower heat, and simmer for 5 minutes, stirring most of the time.
2. Add butter and the first four cheeses; cook until the cheeses are partially melted, about 3 minutes.
3. In a large pot of rapidly boiling salted water cook the spaghetti until al dente, or slightly resistant to the bite. Drain the spaghetti; toss with the olive oil and pour into a large serving bowl.
4. Cover the hot pasta with the cheese sauce and top with the Parmesan cheese. Serve immediately.

Chunky Tomato Mushroom Sauce
Preparation Time: 30 minutes • Serves 6

2 cups sliced portabella mushrooms
1 tablespoon olive oil, to sauté
1–2 clove garlic, minced
One 8-ounce can plain tomato sauce
One 28-ounce can plum tomatoes coarsely chopped
Salt and freshly ground pepper, to taste
¼ cup chopped fresh basil, or 2 teaspoons basil puree
½ cup Parmesan cheese

1. In a large skillet sauté the mushrooms in olive oil for 5–10 minutes. Add garlic and sauté a few minutes more.
2. Add tomato sauce and tomatoes. Season with salt, pepper, and basil. Cook for 20 minutes over medium heat until sauce has thickened. Stir in Parmesan cheese.
3. Serve over freshly cooked pasta.

Sautéed Broccoli and Garlic

Preparation Time: 20 minutes • Serves 6

1 bunch broccoli, trimmed, peeled, and cut into 3-inch
  pieces
1 tablespoon olive oil
3 cloves garlic, thinly sliced

1. Rinse broccoli and steam over rapidly boiling water for 5–10 minutes, or until the broccoli is tender crisp and easily pierced with a knife.

2. Rinse in very cold water and drain well. At this point you could store the broccoli in a plastic bag in the refrigerator until ready to sauté.

3. Heat olive oil in a large skillet over medium heat and quickly sauté garlic until golden brown. Add broccoli and stir-fry until broccoli is heated and garlic and oil are distributed throughout. Serve immediately.

Focaccia with Sage and Rosemary

Focaccia is a rustic, dimpled bread only about ½-inch thick that is found all over Italy with many different seasonings. This simple version can be cut in wedges and served with the spaghetti.

Preparation Time: 30 minutes • Rising Time: 3–4 hours • Baking Time: 25 minutes • Makes 1 large round bread

1 tablespoon active dry yeast
1¼ cups warm (not hot) water
1 tablespoon olive oil
1 teaspoon salt
1 tablespoon dried sage
1 teaspoon dried rosemary
1 tablespoon chopped sun-dried tomatoes, packed in oil
  and drained
1½ cups whole wheat flour
1–1½ cups all-purpose flour
Olive oil, for brushing surface
¼ teaspoon each sage and rosemary, for sprinkling on top

1. Dissolve yeast in warm water in a large bowl. Stir in olive oil, salt, herbs, and tomatoes. Add the whole wheat flour a cup at a time, beating with a whisk until well blended. Using a wooden spoon, stir in the all-purpose flour ½ cup at a time until the mixture comes together in a ball. Knead on a floured surface for 10 minutes until the dough is smooth and elastic.

2. Form dough into a ball and place in an oiled bowl. Cover loosely and let dough rise for 1–2 hours, or until double in bulk.

3. Punch dough down and knead a few times. Coat a 10-inch pie pan or 12-inch pizza pan with vegetable cooking spray; pat or roll dough to fit in the pan. Cover pan with a damp towel and let dough rise for 30 minutes.

4. With your fingertips poke dimples over the entire surface of the dough. Cover again and let rise for another 2 hours.

5. Preheat oven to 400°F.

6. Brush dough lightly with olive oil, sprinkle with sage and rosemary, and bake for 25 minutes. Spray with water a few times in the beginning of the baking period.

7. Remove Focaccia from the baking pan and cool on a rack. Serve warm or at room temperature.

Stewed Oranges and Apricots

We were first served this delicious concoction along with oatmeal, warmed on a wood stove, as part of a vast breakfast spread at a wonderful old Adirondack mountain camp.

Preparation Time: 1 hour • Makes 2½ cups

2 oranges, thinly sliced in rounds, seeded and cut in quarters
1 cup dried apricots, cut in quarters
1½ cups dried prunes
3 lemon slices
3 cups water
1 cinnamon stick
4 whole cloves
¼ cup sugar

Combine the fruits and spices in a large, heavy saucepan. Add water and bring to a boil. Reduce heat and simmer for 20 minutes, stirring occasionally. Add sugar and cook another 10 minutes. Serve warm with oatmeal. Chill the leftovers and serve over vanilla frozen yogurt.

Hot Homemade Cocoa

Jack is the "cocoa man" in the family. He produces this steaming drink on cold mornings and for cross-country skiers. Try mixing a half mug of this cocoa with a half mug of coffee for a great morning drink.

Preparation Time: 15 minutes • Serves 4

⅓ cup unsweetened cocoa powder
½ cup sugar
Dash salt
⅓ cup hot water
4 cups skim milk, or 4 cups water and 1⅓ cups skim milk powder
1 teaspoon vanilla

1. In a large saucepan combine the cocoa, sugar, and salt. Add hot water and cook over medium heat, stirring often, for 2 minutes.
2. Add the milk and heat through but do not boil. Beat with a rotary mixer until foamy. Serve at once in mugs.

Aprés Ski Snacks

Preparation Time: 15 minutes • Makes small snacks for 10 people

10 slices sturdy, whole grain bread
⅓ cup light mayonnaise
⅓ cup plain nonfat yogurt
2 tablespoons light sour cream
1 medium onion, finely chopped
¼ cup freshly grated Parmesan cheese

1. Preheat broiler. Arrange bread slices on a large baking sheet. Mix together the mayonnaise, yogurt, sour cream, and onion; spread about 2 tablespoons on each bread slice. Sprinkle with cheese and cut each piece of bread into quarters.

2. Broil 6 inches from the flame for a few minutes until the tops are lightly browned. Arrange on a platter and pass around to the hungry crowd.

Note: This recipe can easily be multiplied.

Stifado

Stifado is a hearty, spicy Greek stew with many variations.

Preparation Time: 30 minutes • Cooking time: 3 hours • Serves 8

1 tablespoon butter
1 tablespoon olive oil
3 pounds lean stewing beef
2½ pounds small white onions, peeled, or 2 pounds small whole frozen onions
One 6-ounce can tomato paste
½ cup red wine
2 tablespoon red wine vinegar
1 tablespoon brown sugar
1 clove garlic, minced
1 bay leaf
1 small cinnamon stick
½ teaspoon whole cloves
¼ teaspoon ground cumin
2 tablespoons currants (optional)
Salt and freshly ground pepper, to taste

1. Heat the butter and oil in a large Dutch oven or heavy kettle. Add the meat and stir with the butter and oil just to coat, but not brown. Arrange the onions over the meat.

2. Mix the tomato paste, wine, vinegar, sugar, and garlic together and pour over the onions and meat. Spread the bay leaf, cinnamon stick, cloves, cumin, and currants over the top.

3. Bring the stew to a boil, reduce heat and simmer covered for 3 hours or until the meat is very tender. Do not stir the stew as it cooks, but adjust the heat so it doesn't burn on the bottom. Remove the cinnamon stick and bay leaf.

4. Stir the stew as you serve it.

Tips: ■ To keep the onions from falling apart, make an X in the root end of each with a sharp knife.

■ If the stew bubbles while cooking, invert a plate on top of the ingredients to prevent excess movement.

Baked Alaska

Baked Alaska is an all-time great dessert that is fairly easy to make ahead, spectacular to serve, and a joy to eat. To save time, use a store-bought sponge cake for the base.

Preparation Time: 30–40 minutes • Cake Baking Time: 25–30 minutes • Serves 12

Sponge Cake

½ cup skim milk
1 cup all-purpose flour
1 teaspoon baking powder
¼ teaspoon salt
2 eggs
2 egg whites
¾ cup sugar
1 teaspoon vanilla

Meringue

6 egg whites
½ teaspoon cream of tartar
¼ teaspoon salt
¾ cup superfine sugar (pulse regular granulated sugar in a food processor for a few seconds with metal blade)
1 teaspoon vanilla

Filling

½–1 gallon chocolate frozen yogurt, or your favorite flavor of chocolate mixed ice cream, softened ("cookies and cream" is good)
½ pint raspberry sherbet, slightly softened
¼ cup toasted sliced almonds
1 pint vanilla frozen yogurt

Bittersweet Sauce, for topping (see recipe on page 99)

To make the cake:

1. Preheat oven to 350°F.

2. Heat the milk in a small saucepan over low heat until bubbles form around the edges. Remove from heat and set aside.

3. Sift together the flour, baking powder, and salt and set aside. In the large bowl of an electric mixer beat the eggs and egg whites at high speed until foamy and lemon-colored. This will take about 5 minutes; be patient.

4. Gradually add sugar and continue beating for another 5 minutes.

5. Add flour mixture and beat at low speed just until blended. Then beat in the milk and vanilla until just combined. Pour batter into a sprayed and floured 9-inch round cake pan and bake for 25–30 minutes until a cake tester comes out clean.

6. Cool cake 10 minutes in pan, then remove from pan and cool completely on a wire rack. The cake will be about 1-inch high.

To make the meringue:

1. Beat egg whites in a large bowl at high speed until foamy. Add cream of tartar and salt and continue beating until soft peaks form. Gradually add the sugar a tablespoon at a time, beating all the while until stiff peaks form. The meringue should be thick and glossy. Beat in the vanilla and set aside.

To assemble:

1. Set the cake on a 12-inch freezer and ovenproof plate, or a cardboard cake round from the bakery. Spread a 1-inch layer of chocolate ice cream or frozen yogurt on the cake. Mound the sherbet on the center of the ice cream, leaving a 1-inch edge; sprinkle with almonds and cover completely with the vanilla frozen yogurt.

2. Spread the meringue over the ice cream and cake, all the way down to the plate. No cake should show. The layer of meringue should be at least 1 inch thick. Place the entire dessert in the freezer. When it is frozen, lightly cover it with plastic wrap (unless it is slightly sticky, then leave it alone). It will keep well for at least a week.

3. About 30 minutes before serving, take the Alaska out of the freezer to thaw slightly.

4. Preheat oven to 500°F.

5. Bake until tips of meringue brown, about 4 or 5 minutes. Serve immediately with Bittersweet Sauce on the side.

Big Birthday Weekend

Birthdays should be big days. Sometimes we enjoy celebrating with a group of friends of all ages. Since I am not good at cooking and celebrating simultaneously, I have chosen dinner recipes that can be done before the party begins. We try to have un-birthday presents for small hands to open, so that the birthday person can savor opening his or her gifts leisurely and without help. It is not uncommon to find a suspicious small hole poked in the seductively mountainous top of this birthday cake. Try keeping idle hands, both small and large, busy decorating cupcakes with all the colorful toppings you can assemble. *P.W.*

Saturday
Birthday Dinner
Smoked Bluefish Spread* with Toasted Bread Rounds • Crudités with Salsa Verde*
Chilled Boiled Shrimp with Hot Sauce
Chicken with Wild Rice and Cherries*
Green and Orange Salad* • Crisp Sourdough Rolls
Featherweight Cupcakes*
Mountainous Birthday Cake with Boiled Icing*

Sunday
Breakfast/Brunch
Apple Juice and Grapefruit Juice
Individual Omelettes* with Assorted Fillings
Wheat Toast with Honey or All-Fruit Spreads
Cinnamon-Flavored Coffee

*recipe included

THINGS TO DO AHEAD

THE WEEKEND BEFORE

- Bake Cupcakes and Birthday Cake; cover with plastic wrap and store in freezer

THURSDAY

- Wash, spin, and store lettuce for Green and Orange Salad

FRIDAY

- Wash and prepare vegetables for Crudités
- Poach chicken
- Assemble Chicken with Wild Rice and Cherries; refrigerate covered
- Clean and boil Shrimp
- Prepare Smoked Bluefish Spread
- Prepare Salsa Verde

SPECIALTY ITEMS NEEDED

- Dried cherries

WEEKEND WORK PLAN

SATURDAY MORNING

- Frost and hide Birthday Cake and Cupcakes
- Prepare Omelette Fillings
- Cut up Oranges for Salad
- Prepare Salad Dressing

SATURDAY AFTERNOON

- Arrange Crudités on platter; cover with plastic wrap and refrigerate
- Arrange Chilled Boiled Shrimp; cover and refrigerate

SATURDAY EVENING

- Bake Chicken with Wild Rice and Cherries
- Assemble Green and Orange Salad
- Warm rolls
- Just before bed, set up coffee and juice area

SUNDAY MORNING

- Complete breakfast area set-up
- Cook Individual Omelettes

Smoked Bluefish Spread

Pile this spread in a favorite pottery bowl and surround it with toasted bread rounds. It has become one of our "house specialties."

Preparation Time: 20 minutes • Serves 8

1 pound smoked bluefish fillet
6 ounces light cream cheese, softened
1 tablespoon unsalted butter (at room temperature)
2 teaspoons bottled horseradish
1 tablespoon minced red onion
2 teaspoons Dijon mustard
Dash of Tabasco sauce
Freshly ground pepper, to taste
Finely chopped red onion, for garnish

1. Remove skin from fish. Check to make sure that no bones remain. Trim the hard surface from the skin side of the fish.

2. Cut fish into cubes and add to a food processor bowl with all the other ingredients. Using the metal blade, process until you have a smooth puree. Season to taste with salt and pepper.

3. Scoop into a brightly colored bowl and garnish with chopped red onion.

Salsa Verde

Keep a jar of this lovely deep green sauce in the refrigerator. It is *delicious*.

Preparation Time: 10 minutes • Makes 1 cup

2 green onions, chopped
1 clove garlic, chopped
½ cup chopped fresh parsley
3 anchovy fillets, drained
⅓ cup fresh lemon juice
⅓ cup extra-virgin olive oil
2 tablespoons capers, drained
Kale, for garnish

1. Combine all ingredients except the capers in a blender or food processor with metal blade. Process until ingredients are well blended. Stir in capers and transfer to serving bowl.

2. Cover a large glass plate with kale and arrange crudités in an attractive, colorful cirle, leaving space in the center for the bowl of the Salsa Verde.

CRUDITÉS SUGGESTIONS

- Small white mushroom caps
- Red pepper slices
- Green pepper slices
- Yellow pepper slices
- Cauliflower florets
- Broccoli florets
- Baby carrots
- Snow peas
- Zucchini circles

Chicken with Wild Rice and Cherries

This is a slightly modified version of an excellent casserole created by Princeton, New Jersey's wonderful catering company, Main Street. It can be prepared in advance and reheated when needed. For variety, try replacing the dried cherries with dried cranberries.

Preparation Time: 1½ hours • Baking Time: 45 minutes • Serves 8

1 cup raw wild rice
4 tablespoons butter
4 tablespoons flour
2½ cups chicken stock
½ pound mushrooms sliced
  (about 2 cups)
1 teaspoon lemon juice
1 tablespoon minced shallots
¾ cup half-and-half or evaporated skim milk
Pinch ground nutmeg
Salt, to taste
2 cups cooked, cubed boneless chicken breast
½ cup dried cherries (available at specialty food stores)

1. Rinse and drain wild rice. Place rice in a saucepan with 2½ cups water. Bring to a boil, cover, lower heat and simmer for 1 hour, until tender. Drain.

2. Preheat oven to 350°F.

3. To make the sauce, melt 3 tablespoons of the butter in a medium-size saucepan; add flour and blend. Whisk in stock, and let simmer for 15 minutes.

4. Melt the remaining tablespoon of butter in a medium-size skillet. Add the mushrooms and lemon juice. When the mushrooms are tender, add the shallots and continue to cook until most of the liquid has evaporated. Add the mushroom mixture to the sauce. Add the half-and-half, nutmeg, salt, and pepper. Continue to simmer for 15 minutes.

5. Blend chicken, cherries, rice, and sauce in a casserole. Cover loosely and bake for 45 minutes.

Green and Orange Salad

This crisp colorful salad is a perfect partner for the Chicken with Wild Rice and Cherries.

Preparation Time: 30 minutes • Chilling Time: 2 hours • Serves 8

2 cups fresh orange sections
1 red onion, thinly sliced and separated into rings
¼ cup red wine vinegar
¼ cup extra-virgin olive oil
2 tablespoons finely chopped parsley
2 bunches watercress, tough stems removed
6 cups mixed salad lettuce (Bibb, Romaine, or leaf), coarsely torn

1. In a small bowl combine orange sections with onion rings and set aside.

2. Whisk together vinegar and oil and pour over orange/onion mixture. Sprinkle with parsley and chill for 2 hours, tossing occasionally.

3. When ready to serve, toss watercress with lettuce in a large shallow bowl. Spread greens evenly over bottom of bowl and carefully arrange oranges and onions on top. Drizzle dressing over all and serve immediately.

Mountainous Birthday Cake with Boiled Icing

This very tall, spectacular-looking birthday cake was a tradition when I was growing up. By the second day, if any is left, the icing develops a crunchy outer layer that shatters when cut. As one who usually loves a variety of textures, colors, and flavors, I can't explain my love of this sweet white cake. It's delicious and worthy of a special event! Decorate it with fresh edible flowers or a bunch of tall, slender, brightly colored tapers.

Preparation Time: 30 minutes • Baking Time: 30–35 minutes • Makes one 9-inch double layer cake

½ cup vegetable shortening
1½ cups sugar
4 egg yolks, well beaten (save the egg whites for the icing)
1 teaspoon vanilla
3 cups sifted cake flour
4 teaspoon baking powder
½ teaspoon salt
1¼ cups skim milk

1. Preheat oven to 375°F.
2. Coat two 9-inch round cake pans with vegetable cooking spray. Beat shortening and sugar together in a large bowl until light and fluffy. Add egg yolks and vanilla; continue beating until well mixed.
3. Sift flour, baking powder, and salt together into a medium-size bowl. Add the flour to the egg mixture, alternating with the milk, and stirring between each addition. Stir until the batter is smooth.
4. Pour batter into the two pans and bake for 30–35 minutes or until the cake is lightly golden, separates from the edge of the pan, and springs back in the center when lightly touched.
5. Cool layers for 10 minutes in the pans on cooling racks. Remove from pans and cool completely.

Boiled Icing

2 cups sugar
¾ cup water
1 tablespoon light corn syrup
5 egg whites, gently warmed (or pasteurized egg whites)*
2 tablespoons confectioners' sugar
1 teaspoon vanilla

1. Boil sugar, water, and corn syrup in a large uncovered saucepan without stirring over medium heat. Cook until the syrup spins a thread,** beginning at 230°F, and remove from heat. While the syrup is cooking, beat the egg whites with an electric mixer until stiff peaks form; beat in the confectioners' sugar.
2. Slowly pour the boiling syrup over the egg whites, beating constantly. Add vanilla. When the beaters leave tracks in the icing, it is stiff enough to spread.

Note on eggs: If you are concerned about using uncooked eggs, use the 7-minute method: Place all ingredients except vanilla in the top of a double boiler, over 1 inch of simmering water on medium heat. Beat constantly with an electric mixer for about 7 minutes until the beaters leave a track. Add vanilla.

**Note on sugar syrup threads:* Stir the syrup with a wooden spoon; hold the spoon over the pan. If a coarse thread hangs down from the spoon, the syrup is at the crucial, thread-spinning stage. Be careful not to burn the syrup.

To assemble cake:

Turn one layer of cake upside down and place on a large plate. Cover with about a third of the icing (it will be ½ to 1-inch thick). Center the other cake on the iced layer; spread top with a thick layer of icing. Ice the sides.

Featherweight Cupcakes

These delicate little cakes have a delicious hint of orange. Spread them with the light cream cheese frosting and keep cool until ready to decorate.

Preparation Time: 30 minutes • Baking Time: 16–18 minutes • Makes 12 cupcakes

1 cup cake flour
½ cup sugar
1½ teaspoons baking soda
¼ teaspoon salt
2 egg yolks
1 tablespoon grated orange rind
⅓ cup freshly squeezed orange juice
2 tablespoons vegetable oil
4 egg whites
¼ teaspoon cream of tartar

Frosting
6 ounces light cream cheese
1 tablespoon orange juice
1 tablespoon honey

Decorations
Raisins
Chopped fruit
Jellybeans
Chopped nuts

1. Preheat oven to 325°F.
2. Sift flour, sugar, baking soda, and salt together in a medium-size bowl. Make a well in the center. Whisk together egg yolks, orange rind, orange juice, and vegetable oil; pour into well. Beat until thoroughly blended.
3. In a separate bowl, with clean beaters, whip the egg whites and cream of tartar until they are very stiff. Gently fold the egg whites into the batter, a cupful at a time. Mix only until the whites and batter are incorporated; excessive mixing may cause the whites to collapse.
4. Spoon batter into paper-lined muffin tins up to the top; bake immediately. Check the cupcakes after about 15 minutes; they are done when toothpick inserted in the center comes out clean. Cool on wire racks. Cakes will puff up during baking and settle down when cooling. Tops will be bumpy.
5. To make frosting, mix together cream cheese, orange juice, and honey, and spread on cake tops. Top with decorations.

Individual Omelettes

Prepare the omelette fillings ahead of time and keep covered in small serving bowls in the refrigerator. When ready to cook, arrange fillings attractively and encourage guests to make imaginative combinations. Select two or three willing guests to take turns as omelette chefs.

Preparation Time: 5–10 minutes • Makes 1 omelette

2–3 eggs
1 tablespoon water
Salt and pepper, to taste

1. In a small bowl whisk together the eggs, water, and seasonings.
2. Heat a 7 or 8-inch skillet or omelette pan over medium-high heat; coat pan with vegetable cooking spray. Pour in egg mixture and cook, gently lifting cooked portions to allow uncooked mixture to flow underneath. Carefully shake pan to keep the omelette from sticking. Continue to shake pan and lift omelette edges until no liquid remains but the top of the omelette is still creamy.
3. Spoon 2–3 tablespoons of selected filling down the center of the omelette, in line with the pan's handle. Fold omelette and slide onto a warm plate.

OMELETTE FILLING IDEAS

- Shredded low-fat cheese: cheddar, Swiss, Monterey Jack, or crumbled feta or goat cheese
- Chopped tomatoes, green onions, peppers, spinach, or avocado
- Sautéed chopped onions, zucchini, or sliced mushrooms
- Chopped parsley, alfalfa sprouts
- Caviar
- Snipped fresh herbs

SPRING WEEKENDS

Although greatly anticipated, spring is almost a non-season in New England. Its arrival is subtle; its unfolding serene. There are no festivals to celebrate the profusion of brightly colored flowering shrubs as in more southern climates. However, the pleasure is intense as water begins to drip off icicles, brown grass appears in ever-growing patches beneath the soiled snow, the air softens, tree buds swell, and sturdy daffodil spears poke through matted, dried leaves. When the sap buckets appear on the maple trees, we know that the back of winter is broken, even though there may be yet another storm. The realization that the days are growing longer brings the certainty that warmth lies ahead. Frozen ground gives way to mud and with it comes a feeling of anticipation as the grass turns green, bulbs open, and the shadblow blooms. It is a time to walk in a gentle rain, clean out the garden, work in the yard, and just sit outside in the sunshine. It is time to put away the stew pots, bring out the grill, go on a picnic, eat fresh asparagus, and enjoy lighter meals.

Singles in the City

One of the joys of living in a city is the abundance of interesting food stores. Take advantage of these shops when friends come to visit and create an array of lunchtime pleasures for when your guests arrive. Enjoy the variety of ethnic bakeries, delis, and coffee shops. *E.S.*

~~~~~~~~~~~~~~~~~~~~

Saturday
Lunch

Sandwich Bar with assorted breads and crusty whole wheat rolls from your favorite bakery
and a selection of sliced cheeses, meats, and marinated vegetables
from a neighborhood deli, served with several mustards
Cookies • Fruit

Dinner

Tandoori Chicken* • Red Lentils* • Basmati Rice*
Chapatis (an Indian flat bread) • Cucumber Raita* • Mango Chutney
Sherbet with Orange Slices*

Sunday
Brunch

Breakfast Bread Basket, including assorted breakfast breads, rolls, and Meg's Scones*
Raisin Walnut Bread (from a bakery) • Sweet Butter, Marscapone Cheese, Marmalades, and Jams
Fresh Sliced Citrus Fruit Sprinkled with Finely Chopped Cranberries
Swiss Chocolate Coffee

*recipe included

THINGS TO DO AHEAD

THE WEEKEND BEFORE

■ Make and freeze Meg's Scones

SPECIALTY ITEMS NEEDED

■ Chapatis
■ Mango chutney
■ Marscapone cheese
■ Raisin walnut bread

WEEKEND WORK PLAN

FRIDAY EVENING

■ Marinate Tandoori Chicken
■ Slice citrus fruit for Sunday brunch and store covered in refrigerator

SATURDAY MORNING

■ Thaw Scones
■ Shop at bakery for cookies, rolls, bread, and chapatis
■ Go to deli for sandwich makings
■ Arrange Sandwich Bar

SATURDAY AFTERNOON

■ Do something fun in the city!

SATURDAY EVENING

■ Grate and chill cucumbers for Raita
■ Cook Tandoori Chicken
■ Cook Basmati Rice
■ Cook Red Lentils
■ Prepare Cucumber Raita
■ Prepare the Sherbet with Orange Slices just before serving

SATURDAY NIGHT

■ Go out dancing

SUNDAY MORNING

■ Arrange brunch table food and enjoy a leisurely meal with the Sunday papers

SUNDAY AFTERNOON

■ Visit a museum

Tandoori Chicken

If you haven't tried this spicy yogurt Indian marinade, you are in for a treat. An added bonus is that much of the work is done ahead. In India this dish would be cooked over coals in a tulip-shaped clay oven called a *Tandoor*.

Preparation Time: 20 minutes • Marinating Time: 24 hours • Cooking Time: 60 minutes • Serves 8

1 medium onion, chopped
6 cloves garlic, minced
3 tablespoons grated gingerroot
3 tablespoons fresh lime juice
1½ cup plain nonfat yogurt
1 tablespoon ground coriander
1 teaspoon ground cumin
1 teaspoon ground turmeric
1 teaspoon garam masala (optional; available in specialty shops)
¼ teaspoon ground nutmeg
¼ teaspoon ground cinnamon
1 teaspoon salt
¼ teaspoon freshly ground pepper
¼ teaspoon ground cayenne pepper
2 tablespoon olive oil
8 chicken thighs or breasts
1 lime, cut into wedges

1. Mix the onion, garlic, ginger, and lime juice together in a large bowl. Add the yogurt, spices, and oil, and stir well. Remove skin from chicken; slash chicken diagonally three times, rinse, and pat dry. Add chicken to the marinade and massage the marinade into the slashes. Cover and refrigerate for 24 hours, turning several times.
2. Preheat oven to 400°F.
3. Remove chicken from the marinade and arrange on a rack in a large roasting pan. Spoon marinade over the top and bake for 45–60 minutes or until very tender. Serve the chicken on a large platter surrounded by lime wedges.

Red Lentils

Kate introduced us to the wonderful, spicy flavor of red lentils which became a staple of her graduate school existence. It's a great accompaniment to Tandoori Chicken, and also makes a delicious meatless meal with basmati rice, chutney, and a cool cucumber raita.

Preparation Time: 30 minutes • Serves 8

2 teaspoons canola oil
½ teaspoon whole cumin seeds
1 clove garlic, minced
1 tablespoon grated gingerroot
½ teaspoon cinnamon
¼ teaspoon ground cloves
¼ teaspoon ground cardamom
¼–½ teaspoon cayenne pepper, according to your taste buds
1 medium onion, chopped
1 ¼ cups red lentils, thoroughly rinsed and drained
1 teaspoon turmeric
½ teaspoon salt
2½ cups water

1. In a large, heavy saucepan, heat oil over medium heat. Add cumin seeds and heat them until they pop. Add garlic, ginger, cinnamon, cloves, cardamom, pepper, onion, and lentils. Cook until the onion is translucent.
2. Add turmeric, salt, and water; bring to a boil. Turn heat down and simmer uncovered until much of the water has evaporated as the lentils bubble slowly, stirring occasionally. This will take about 15 minutes. Serve hot with the chicken.

Basmati Rice

Basmati rice is generally grown in India. This Asian method of cooking rice gives a slightly moist texture.

Preparation Time: 30 minutes • Serves 8

1½ cups basmati rice, rinsed and drained
3 cups water
½ teaspoon salt

In a large, heavy saucepan bring the rice and water to a boil over high heat. Turn heat down very low; tightly cover the pot and cook until water is evaporated and rice is tender, about 20 minutes. Fluff with a fork and serve hot.

Cucumber Raita

A cool, refreshing antidote to the spicy Tandoori.

Preparation Time: 10 minutes • Sitting Time: 30 minutes • Serves 8

4 cucumbers, peeled and grated
1 teaspoon ground cumin
1 tablespoon cider vinegar
1 teaspoon horseradish
1–1½ cups plain nonfat yogurt

Let the grated cucumber sit in a medium-size bowl in the refrigerator for about 30 minutes. Drain off any water that collects in the bowl and add the cumin, vinegar, horseradish, and yogurt; stir well. Serve cold with the chicken.

Orange Sherbet with Orange Slices

I discovered this simple, elegant dessert years ago and it has been a mainstay ever since. If you are in a rush, canned mandarin oranges are also good, but I prefer the taste of fresh oranges.

Preparation Time: 15 minutes • Serves 8

½ gallon orange sherbet
3 large oranges
1–2 tablespoons Cointreau (optional)

1. In the morning, or whenever you have time, peel the oranges and separate the sections from the membrane. Squeeze the excess juice from the membrane over the sections and store in a covered bowl in the refrigerator until ready to use.

2. Use pretty glass dessert dishes, or large wine glasses, and serve several scoops of orange sherbet in each. Spoon the orange sections and juice over the sherbet; top with a splash of Cointreau if desired.

Note: After peeling and removing the outer white membrane, you can separate orange sections efficiently by slicing along a sectional membrane toward the heart of the orange; shift the angle of the blade and continue slicing toward the outer edge.

Meg's Scones

Meg serves these wonderfully light scones to her friends in the city. We love them too.

Preparation Time: 20 minutes • Makes 8 scones

2⅔ cups all-purpose flour
½ teaspoon salt
1 tablespoon baking powder
½ cup sugar
½ cup unsalted butter
¼ cup currants
⅔ cup skim milk

1. Preheat oven to 425°F.
2. Combine dry ingredients in a medium-size bowl. With a pastry blender cut in the butter until the mixture resembles coarse crumbs.
3. Add the currants.
4. Add the milk and mix well with a fork. Knead the dough ten times. Roll into a 1-inch thick circle and cut into eight wedges. Separate the wedges and bake on an ungreased baking sheet for 12 minutes.

Cinnamon Oat Scones

Add 1 teaspoon cinnamon; substitute 1¼ cups oats for 1 cup of the all-purpose flour. Grind the oats slightly in a food processor before adding.

Whole Wheat Scones

Vary the flavor by substituting whole wheat pastry flour for 1 cup of the all-purpose flour.

The Family Descends

Frequently our children come home accompanied by friends, families, and pets. The kitchen has become the place to gather, so I suggest the following menu with this in mind. Family ties are strengthened by sharing the preparation and consumption of new experiments and old favorites. Most of the recipes I have included are quite simple and could be prepared partially in advance. Choose someone responsible, however, to watch over Friday night's soup and Sunday morning's Big Breakfast Popover — they need careful attention. *P.W.*

Friday
Dinner
Pappa al Pomodoro* (Bread and Tomato Soup)
Roasted Rosemary Chicken*
Chilled Couscous with Radishes and Pine Nuts*
Garden Salad
Fresh Pears • Crunchy Nut Clusters*

Saturday
Breakfast
Freshly Squeezed Orange Juice
Eggs of Your Choice
Eternal Bran Muffins*

Lunch
Chicken and Watercress Sandwiches on Whole Wheat Bread
(use the leftover chicken from Friday night)

Dinner
White Chili* served with sliced black olives,
chopped plum tomatoes, shredded red leaf lettuce, chopped
green onions, shredded light cheddar cheese, and sour
cream substitute • Low-Salt Blue Corn Chips
Cranapple Walnut Cake*

Sunday
Breakfast
Honeydew Slices • Big Breakfast Popover*
Hot Cocoa • Cinnamon-flavored Coffee

recipe included

THINGS TO DO AHEAD

THE WEEKEND BEFORE

- Make Crunchy Nut Clusters and store in freezer
- Make Couscous and store in refrigerator
- Prepare Eternal Bran Muffin batter and store in refrigerator

WEDNESDAY

- Cook chicken breasts for White Chili (serve some for dinner and save what's needed for chili)

THURSDAY

- Make White Chili
- Wash, dry, spin, and store lettuce to accompany Chili
- Bake Cranapple Walnut Cake

WEEKEND WORK PLAN

FRIDAY MORNING

- Thaw Crunchy Nut Clusters

FRIDAY EVENING

- Roast Rosemary Chicken
- Prepare Pappa al Pomodoro
- Complete Chilled Couscous; toss and serve
- Just before bed, set up coffee and juice area

SATURDAY MORNING

- Bake Eternal Bran Muffins
- Cook eggs, or have the guests cook their own

SATURDAY NOON

- Set up sandwich makings

SATURDAY EVENING

- Warm White Chili
- Arrange chili toppings and chips
- Just before bed, set up coffee and juice area

SUNDAY MORNING

- Slice melons
- Prepare cocoa
- Prepare Big Breakfast Popover

Pappa al Pomodoro (Bread and Tomato Soup)

This soup is proof that the whole is greater than the sum of its parts. It was taught to me by a young American cook in Florence and has been a favorite for years. You will need time but not a great deal of concentration. It is perfect to cook with a kitchen full of chattering guests. Use the finest olive oil you can find and choose an excellent country bread, semolina if possible. This soup is delicious at room temperature.

Preparation Time: 1 hour • Serves 6

¾ cup extra-virgin olive oil
2 cloves garlic, peeled and chopped
1 bunch fresh sage, stems removed and chopped, or 1 generous tablespoon dried sage leaves
1 large loaf day-old country bread, cut into 1-inch cubes
3 pounds tomatoes, peeled and seeded, or two 28-ounce cans imported crushed or pureed tomatoes
Coarse salt and freshly ground pepper, to taste
Grated Parmesan cheese for garnish

1. Heat the oil in a large heavy saucepan or kettle over medium-high heat. Briefly sauté the garlic. Add the bread and sage to the pan. Using a wooden spoon, stir until bread turns a golden brown.

2. Add the tomatoes and season with salt and pepper.

3. Bring to a boil and cook for 5 minutes, stirring constantly. Add just enough cold water to cover the tomato/bread mixture. Reduce heat, cover, and simmer, stirring frequently over low heat for at least 30 minutes, until bread has absorbed tomatoes and becomes mushy. If soup is too thick, add a bit of water.

4. To serve, ladle into individual bowls and garnish with grated cheese.

Roasted Rosemary Chicken

Bill and J.B. prepare this simple and superb dish. It will fill your kitchen with a wonderful warm aroma that will welcome weary travelers. Roast two chickens to feed six and be sure to have leftovers for sandwiches on Saturday.

Preparation Time: 20 minutes • Roasting Time: 1–1½ hours • Serves 4

One 4- to 5-pound roasting chicken
3 cloves garlic, crushed
8 rosemary sprigs, or 1 tablespoon dried rosemary
2 lemons
Salt

1. Preheat oven to 400°F.
2. Thoroughly wash and dry the chicken; rub salt inside the chest cavity. Rub garlic outside and inside the chicken. Slip thin slivers of one of the garlic cloves under the chicken skin; drop the remaining two cloves into the cavity.
3. Rub entire chicken with rosemary, inside and out. If you are using rosemary sprigs, slip one under skin on each breast. Place three of the remaining sprigs in the cavity.
4. Split one of the lemons and squeeze juice over the inside and outside of the chicken. Place squeezed halves in cavity.
5. Truss chicken and place on rack in roasting pan. Roast chicken, basting occasionally, until done and the juices run clear (1–1½ hours).
6. Cool to room temperature and serve garnished with second lemon (sliced) and remaining rosemary sprigs.

Chilled Couscous with Radishes and Pine Nuts

Preparation Time: 30 minutes • Serves 6

¾ cup chicken stock
1½ cups water
1½ cups uncooked couscous (one 10-ounce package)
¾ cup orange juice
1 tablespoon grated orange rind
½ cup chopped fresh parsley
3 tablespoons extra-virgin olive oil
3 tablespoons cider vinegar
1½ cups thinly sliced radishes
⅓ cup pine nuts, toasted
Salt and freshly ground pepper, to taste

1. In a medium saucepan bring chicken stock and water to a boil; add couscous slowly, stirring constantly, until all liquid has been absorbed. Remove from heat and let stand 2 minutes.

2. Turn the couscous onto a large baking sheet; spread evenly and cool to room temperature. When cool, separate any clumps and transfer to a large mixing bowl. Add ½ cup of the orange juice, orange rind, and parsley and toss. (Couscous can be refrigerated at this point for a day or two if you like.)

3. Before serving whisk together the remaining ¼ cup orange juice, oil, and vinegar and toss with couscous mixture. Add radishes and pine nuts and toss again. Season to taste and serve.

Crunchy Nut Clusters

These delightful delicacies are the creation of Florida cook Charlotte Balcomb Lane. They freeze well and are perfect for packed lunches.

Preparation Time: 20 minutes • Baking Time: 8–10 minutes • Makes 2 dozen clusters

2 cups whole unsalted cashews, almonds, or walnut halves, lightly toasted
½ cup wheat germ
1 cup golden raisins
1 cup dried apricots, chopped
½ cup rolled oats (quick or old-fashioned)
¼ cup firmly packed brown sugar
⅔ cup light corn syrup
¼ cup smooth peanut butter

1. Preheat oven to 350°F. Coat a baking sheet with vegetable cooking spray.

2. Combine nuts, wheat germ, raisins, apricots, and oats in a large bowl and set aside.

3. In a small heavy saucepan combine sugar, corn syrup, and peanut butter. Bring to a boil over medium heat, stirring constantly. Immediately pour over nut mixture, stirring until well coated. Drop mixture by rounded tablespoonfuls onto the cookie sheet.

4. Bake 8 to 10 minutes or until golden brown; be careful not to overcook. Cool on wire rack.

Eternal Bran Muffins

We call these moist tender muffins eternal because the batter used to make them can be stored in the refrigerator for several weeks without losing any flavor. Bake them as you need them adding dates, apples, chopped nuts, currants, raisins or other fruit. You might want to write the date on the container — "eternal" may be a bit of an exaggeration (two weeks is probably more like it!).

Preparation Time: 20 minutes • Baking Time: 15–20 minutes • Makes 4 dozen

6 cups 100% bran cereal
2 cups boiling water
1 cup canola oil
1 cup granulated sugar
1 cup brown sugar
4 eggs, beaten
1 quart buttermilk
5 cups whole wheat pastry flour or all-purpose flour, or a combination of the two
5 teaspoons baking soda
2 teaspoons salt
2 cups fruit and/or nuts of your choice (chopped dates, apples, chopped nuts, currants, or raisins)

1. Preheat oven to 375°F.

2. Coat the inside of muffin tins with vegetable cooking spray.

3. Put 2 cups of bran cereal in a medium-size bowl and cover with the boiling water. Mix in oil; let cool.

4. In a large bowl mix together the rest of the cereal with sugar, eggs, and buttermilk. Add flour, baking soda, and salt. Combine all ingredients except fruit and/or nuts. If you are using all the batter, add them now; if not add only a proportional amount. (At this point, you may transfer the mixture to a tightly covered container and store in the refrigerator until ready to add remaining fruit and bake.)

5. Spoon batter into muffin cups about ¾ full; bake for 15 to 20 minutes, or until tester inserted into center of muffin comes out clean. Serve hot.

White Chili

This hearty and healthy chili is a snap to make. Serve it in an earthenware crock surrounded by a collection of your favorite small bowls heaped with the colorful garnishes. The chili can be made well in advance, even a day or two before serving, and reheated.

Preparation Time: 45 minutes • Cooking Time: 15 minutes • Serves 8

Three 20-ounce cans of white kidney (canellini) beans, drained and rinsed
One 13-ounce can low-salt chicken broth
1 tablespoon extra-virgin olive oil
2 large cloves garlic, minced
2 cups chopped onions
1 jalapeño pepper, seeded and minced
One 4-ounce can chopped green chiles
2 teaspoons ground cumin
2 teaspoons dried oregano
¼ teaspoon cinnamon
Hot pepper sauce, to taste
2 whole chicken breasts, cooked and cut into small cubes (about 4 cups)

1. In a heavy kettle combine beans with the chicken stock and heat gently over low heat while you prepare the other ingredients.
2. In a small skillet heat the oil; sauté the garlic until light brown; add onions and cook until soft. Remove from heat. Blend in the chiles and seasonings.
3. Toss chicken cubes with onion/chile mixture and add to beans. Mix gently but thoroughly. Heat, but don't allow to boil, over medium heat for 10–15 minutes.

GARNISHES

- Sliced black olives
- Chopped plum tomatoes
- Chopped green onions (green part only)
- Shredded light cheddar cheese
- Sour cream substitute (½ sour cream, ½ low-fat yogurt)

Cranapple Walnut Cake

This moist rich cake is a delicious step away from the common carrot cake. Serve it warm topped with a dollop of vanilla frozen yogurt.

Preparation Time: 30 minutes • Baking Time: 45 minutes • Serves 8

½ cup light brown sugar
½ cup granulated sugar
1 egg
⅓ cup canola oil
1 cup whole wheat pastry flour or all-purpose flour
½ teaspoon salt
1 teaspoon baking soda
1 teaspoon cinnamon
¼ teaspoon nutmeg
½ cup coarsely cut cranberries
2 cups shredded apples (about 5 medium apples with skins)
1 cup chopped walnuts
Vanilla frozen yogurt

1. Preheat oven to 350°F. Coat the inside of an 8 by 8-inch pan with vegetable cooking spray.
2. Cream sugars and egg together by hand; blend in oil.
3. Combine flour, salt, soda, cinnamon, and nutmeg and add to sugar/egg mixture. Mix by hand. The mixture will be quite stiff.
4. Toss together the cranberries, shredded apples, and walnuts and fold into flour/sugar mixture. Turn into oiled pan and bake for 45 minutes. Cool on a wire rack for 10 minutes; serve warm.

Big Breakfast Popover

This is a cross between a BIG popover and an oven pancake. It makes a spectacular appearance and is very easy to put together. The pan you use is important. If you have a paella pan, or an attractive, large shallow casserole dish, use it. I have relied on my old faithful Pyrex glass baking dish. Just don't choose a deep-sided dish. Determine the capacity of your pan with premeasured cups of water before you start filling it. The pan must hold 3–4 quarts.

Preparation Time: 15 minutes • Baking Time: 20–25 minutes • Serves 4–6

5 tablespoons unsalted butter
4 eggs
1 cup skim milk
1 cup whole wheat pastry or all-purpose flour (or a combination of the two)
1 ¼ teaspoons cinnamon

OPTIONAL TOPPINGS

■ Powdered sugar with a spritz of lemon juice
■ Warm maple syrup
■ Sliced seasonal fruit

1. Preheat oven to 425°F.
2. Place butter in a 3–4 quart casserole and put in hot oven to melt.
3. Beat eggs at high speed in medium mixing bowl. Reduce speed, slowly add milk, and then flour and cinnamon. Beat until thoroughly mixed.
4. Remove pan from oven and pour in batter. Return to oven and bake until puffed and golden brown. Cut in wedges and serve immediately on warm plates with toppings of your choice.

Engagement Celebration with Family and Friends

Celebrating an engagement is a joyous event which also has its elements of stress. This may be the first time the two families get together. So you may be faced with a houseful of people — some of whom you know and love, and some whom you've barely met. Plan carefully and do as much ahead as possible. This festive menu provides many opportunities for advance preparation so you won't spend most of the weekend in the kitchen. *E.S.*

Saturday
Lunch for Assembled Family Members and Friends
"Make Your Own" Sandwich Bar, with sliced tomatoes,
grated carrots and zucchini, and
thinly sliced onions
Gruyére Cheese, Imported Ham, and Sprouts
Mustards
Multigrain Breads
Chilled Flavored Seltzer Water

Family Dinner
Grilled Salmon*
Steamed Fresh Green Beans or Asparagus
Hot and Cold Sesame Noodles*
Raspberry Floating Island*

Sunday
Brunch
Popovers*
Tomato Strata*
Hazelnut Coffee
Fresh Fruit

Afternoon Party
Wedding Cake Cheese* and Pesto Torte*
Assorted Whole Grain Crackers
Cold Salmon with Mustard Sauce* (see page 77)
Northern Italian Lasagna*
Spinach and Arugula Salad with Strawberries and
Lime Dressing* • Chilled Asparagus
Crusty Whole Wheat Rolls
Chocolate Raspberry Torte* • Champagne

recipe included

THINGS TO DO AHEAD

THE WEEKEND BEFORE

- Get out dishes, candles, and vases you will use at the party

THURSDAY

- Cook pasta for Hot and Cold Sesame Noodles; toss with oils and refrigerate
- Bake Popovers and freeze

FRIDAY

- Prepare Wedding Cake Cheese and Pesto Torte; cover with plastic wrap and store in refrigerator
- Prepare Northern Italian Lasagna, but don't bake; refrigerate
- Wash, spin, and store Spinach and Arugula for salad
- Steam and chill asparagus

SPECIALTY ITEMS NEEDED

- One 10-inch removable-bottom cake pan

WEEKEND WORK PLAN

SATURDAY MORNING

- Make Chocolate Raspberry Torte and chill
- Arrange sandwich bar so it's ready as people arrive
- Buy flowers for the party table
- Have someone clean the green beans

SATURDAY AFTERNOON

- Prepare Tomato Strata and store in refrigerator
- Complete Hot and Cold Sesame Noodles
- Make Raspberry Floating Island; complete the dessert and chill in refrigerator

SATURDAY EVENING

- Steam beans
- Grill Salmon; cook extra and chill it for Sunday's party

SUNDAY MORNING

- Remove Tomato Strata from refrigerator
- Thaw Popovers
- Bake Strata
- Warm Popovers

SUNDAY AFTERNOON

- Arrange party table with food
- Bake Northern Italian Lasagna
- Prepare Spinach and Arugula Salad
- Make Mustard Dill Sauce for salmon
- Warm rolls
- Enjoy the party!

Grilled Salmon

Simple but elegant. Cook extra salmon without the tarragon to make Cold Salmon with Mustard Sauce for the buffet on Sunday afternoon.

Preparation Time: 30 minutes • Serves 6–8

1½ pounds salmon fillet
Good-quality olive oil
¼ cup fresh tarragon leaves

1. Rub the salmon fillets with olive oil and sprinkle with tarragon. Grill the salmon 4–5 minutes on each side. Turn gently, as it becomes fragile when cooked. Salmon can be slightly translucent in the center when removed because it will continue to cook once removed from the grill.
2. Cut the salmon into serving pieces and arrange on a platter. Garnish with a few fresh sprigs of tarragon.

Mustard Sauce

2 tablespoons light mayonnaise
½ cup plain nonfat yogurt
¼ cup Dijon mustard
1 tablespoon lemon juice
1 tablespoon minced fresh dill

Mix all ingredients together. This sauce is good served with either hot or cold salmon.

Hot and Cold Sesame Noodles

Preparation time: 30 minutes • Serves 8

¾ pound good-quality Italian spaghetti
1 tablespoon sesame oil
1–2 teaspoons hot chili oil
6 green onions, trimmed, cut on the diagonal into 1-inch
   pieces, and sliced in half lengthwise

Sauce

1 teaspoon cornstarch
½ cup chicken broth
3 tablespoons rice vinegar
3 tablespoons soy sauce
3 tablespoons Dijon mustard
1 tablespoon dark sesame oil

1. In a large kettle of boiling salted water cook the spaghetti until al dente, about 8 minutes. Drain and toss with sesame and chili oils; let cool. Toss with green onions.

2. For the sauce, cook the cornstarch and chicken broth in a small saucepan over medium heat, stirring until the mixture thickens. Whisk in the remaining ingredients and pour over pasta. For a spicier mix, add more hot chili oil. Serve at room temperature.

Raspberry Floating Island

By combining favorite flavors and textures — the sweet, smooth, mellow custard, the airy meringue, and the tart raspberry — we achieve a celestial dessert.

Preparation Time: 30 minutes • Serves 8

Meringue
4 egg whites (at room temperature)
½ cup sugar
½ teaspoon vanilla
1 teaspoon cassis

Custard
3 whole eggs
½ cup sugar
¼ teaspoon salt
4 cups skim milk, warmed
1 teaspoon vanilla
1 pint fresh raspberries
3 tablespoons sugar

1. With an electric mixer beat the egg whites until soft peaks form. Gradually beat in the sugar, a little at a time. Continue beating until stiff peaks form. Add the vanilla and the cassis and mix well.

2. In a large skillet gently heat the milk for the custard until little bubbles form around the edges. Do not let it boil. Drop the egg white mixture by tablespoons into the simmering milk and poach for about 4 minutes, turning once. Make 8 meringues.

With a skimmer or slotted spoon, carefully lift the meringues onto a tea towel. Save the hot milk for the custard.

3. To make custard, in a large heavy saucepan whisk together the eggs and remaining egg whites until they are thick. Add sugar and salt. Slowly add the hot milk, whisking all the time. Cook over low to medium heat, stirring constantly. The eggs will thicken the sauce, but if cooked at too high a temperature they will scramble. Cook until the sauce begins to thicken and is very hot, but not boiling. Remove custard sauce from heat; strain and stir in the vanilla.

4. Cool the custard and strain it into a large serving bowl the shape of a pasta bowl. Float the meringues on top and chill.

5. About 30 minutes before serving, rinse, drain, and slightly mash the raspberries; mix with sugar and let sit to draw the juices. Place several spoonfuls of raspberries in the bottom of each dessert dish. Ladle custard into each dish, swirl raspberries with a spoon, top with a meringue, and await the sighs of pleasure.

Popovers

Popovers must be eaten while they are hot. Happily they can be made ahead, frozen, and reheated for serving on the weekend. They are also delicious hot from the oven. There are many variations, but the basic recipe is great and is a tribute to the many seventh graders I've taught who have run home from school to make them for their families. Use dark-colored non-stick muffins pans since popovers tend to stick in shiny pans.

Preparation Time: 15 minutes • Baking Time: 30 minutes • Makes 12 popovers

1 cup all-purpose flour
¼ teaspoon salt
1 cup low-fat milk
2 tablespoons oil
1 egg
2 egg whites

1. Preheat oven to 450°F. Spray a muffin pan with vegetable cooking spray.

2. Mix the flour and salt together in a large bowl. In another bowl, beat together the milk, oil, egg, and egg whites.

3. Add the milk mixture to the flour and whisk until batter is smooth.

4. Pour batter into the muffin pan so that each cup has about the same amount. Bake for 15 minutes. Turn oven down to 350°F and bake for another 15 minutes. Remove popovers from the pan and enjoy them while they're HOT. Serve with small bits of butter and your favorite jam.

Tomato Strata

Strata make a wonderful breakfast when you have guests because the dish is assembled the day before.

Preparation Time: 30 minutes • Setting Time: Overnight • Baking Time: 1 hour • Serves 6

12 slices sourdough or regular French bread, cut in ½-inch diagonal slices
3 medium ripe tomatoes, sliced
½ cup sliced sun-dried tomatoes (packed in oil and drained), or dried tomatoes plumped with boiling water
1 cup fresh basil leaves, shredded
1–2 tablespoons olive oil
2 cups mixed grated Italian Fontina and Gruyère cheeses
4 eggs
2 egg whites
3 cups evaporated skimmed milk
1 teaspoon dried oregano
¼ teaspoon salt
Freshly ground black pepper
¼ cup freshly grated Parmesan cheese

use sharp cheeses
dry mustard

1. Lightly coat a 2-quart casserole dish with vegetable cooking spray; line the dish with half of the bread slices. Arrange the tomato slices and sun-dried tomatoes over the bread; scatter the basil leaves on top, drizzle with olive oil, and sprinkle grated cheese over all. Lay the remaining bread slices over the cheese and press down.

2. In a large bowl whisk the eggs and egg whites together until they are foamy. Add the milk, oregano, salt, and pepper and mix well. Pour this mixture over the bread. Cover the casserole with plastic wrap and let sit in the refrigerator overnight.

3. Preheat oven to 350°F.

4. Sprinkle the strata with the Parmesan cheese and bake for 45 minutes to 1 hour, or until it is puffy and golden brown. Serve hot!

~~~~~~~~~~~~~~~~~~~

Wedding Cake Cheese

Preparation Time: 15–30 minutes • Makes 20 small servings

3 round soft cheeses of 3 different sizes, such as Brie, Camembert, and Saga Blue
Fresh edible flowers
Assorted crackers

Arrange the cheeses on a doily on a plate in descending sizes, like a wedding cake. Decorate with fresh flowers. Serve at room temperature with toast triangles and plain crackers.

~~~~~~~~~~~~~~~~~~~

Pesto Torte

One of the most wonderful combinations of flavors I've eaten!

Preparation Time: 15–30 minutes • Makes 20 small servings

18 ounces goat cheese, softened
12 ounces light cream cheese, softened
¼ cup feta cheese
½ cup basil pesto
1½ cups sliced sun-dried tomatoes, packed in olive oil and well drained
Assorted plain crackers such as water biscuits

1. On a large round serving plate shape goat cheese into a 1-inch high circle. Spread with a layer of pesto about ⅛-inch thick.

2. Mix the cream cheese and feta together and shape into a smaller circle on top of the pesto layer. Cover with plastic wrap and refrigerate until ready to serve.

3. Spread most of the sun-dried tomatoes on the feta/cream cheese layer. Sprinkle the remaining tomatoes over the entire creation, allowing some to fall on the first tier and sides. Arrange the crackers around the cheeses and serve at room temperature.

Northern Italian Lasagna

Lasagna is not a quick and easy dish to make but this wonderful, creamy version, adapted from the classic lasagna of Bologna, Italy, is worth the time. This dish was inspired by a recipe from a wonderful cookbook by The Junior League of Palo Alto/Mid-Peninsula California called *Private Collection.* It can be made ahead and is easily doubled for larger groups.

Preparation Time: 1 hour • Baking Time: 30 minutes • Makes 1 pan of lasagna/serves 8

12 lasagna noodles or 3 sheets of fresh pasta

Meat Sauce
½ pound lean ground beef
1 medium onion, chopped
3 cloves garlic, minced
2 carrots, peeled and chopped
1 teaspoon olive oil
3 ounces chopped lean ham
½ cup red wine
4 large tomatoes seeded and chopped, or 4 cups frozen or canned tomato chunks
¼ teaspoon salt
2 tablespoons minced fresh parsley
2 tablespoons chopped fresh basil, or 2 teaspoons dried
1 teaspoon oregano
Freshly ground pepper

Creamy Sauce
3 tablespoons butter
3 tablespoons flour
3 cups skim milk
1 cup low-sodium chicken broth
¼ teaspoon nutmeg

¾ cup Parmesan cheese (freshly grated *Parmigiano Reggiano* is best)
1 cup fresh bread crumbs
1 tablespoon butter

1. Cook lasagna noodles according to package directions. Drain until ready for use. (If using fresh pasta, omit this step.)
2. Sauté beef, onions, garlic, and carrots in the olive oil in a large kettle over medium heat. Add ham and cook for 2 minutes. Add remaining meat sauce ingredients, bring to a boil, lower heat, and simmer uncovered for 40 minutes, or until sauce is thick.
3. While sauce is simmering, make the creamy sauce. Melt butter in a medium-size saucepan. Add flour and cook over low heat, stirring constantly for 1 minute. Stir in milk and cook until thickened. Add chicken broth, nutmeg, and cheese and stir until smooth. Remove from heat and set aside for later when assembling the lasagna.

(continued on next page)

4. Preheat oven to 400°F. Coat a 9 by 13-inch pan with vegetable cooking spray.

5. Place a small amount of meat sauce in the bottom of the pan. Cover with a layer of noodles, 1 cup meat sauce, 1⅓ cup creamy sauce, and ⅓ cup bread crumbs. Repeat for 2 more layers. Dot with butter and bake uncovered for 30 minutes or until bubbly. Let sit for a few minutes before cutting into squares and serving.

6. To assemble the lasagna, create an assembly line for yourself in the following order: meat sauce, noodles, creamy sauce, bread crumbs.

Tip: To make fresh bread crumbs, tear a piece of dry bread in quarters. Turn on blender, remove small cover from top, and drop the pieces into the hole with the blender running.

Spinach and Arugula Salad with Strawberries and Lime Dressing

Arugula is a wonderfully spicy-tasting green with an incredible, pungent aroma. Unfortunately it is expensive to buy in the market, but (fortunately for gardeners) it is very easy to grow in the garden. I love fresh strawberries in green salads. Another nice addition to this salad is Italian cannellini beans. Make several bowls of this salad for a crowd.

Preparation Time: 15 minutes • Serves 8

1 pound fresh spinach, washed, drained, and dried with stalk and central stem removed
1 bunch arugula, washed, drained, and dried
1 small red onion, thinly sliced
3 tablespoons canola oil
3 tablespoons fresh lime juice
Salt and freshly ground black pepper, to taste
1 pint fresh strawberries, washed, hulled, and cut in half

1. Tear spinach and arugula into bite-size pieces; place in a large salad bowl with sloping sides. Add the onion and toss lightly with your hands. Whisk together the oil and lime juice; season with salt and pepper. Pour dressing over the salad and toss well.

2. Scatter the strawberries artfully across the top of the salad and serve with a flourish.

Chocolate Raspberry Torte

This delicious cake is unashamedly rich. Some recipes are better left untampered with, and this is one of them. Serve small slices and enjoy every crumb. It has been my daughter Kate's favorite birthday cake since she was old enough to appreciate chocolate. A torte is a many layered cake which uses little or no flour. This one has two layers, and uses ground walnuts instead of flour.

Preparation Time: 30 minutes • Baking Time: 1 hour • Makes one 10-inch cake

6 eggs, separated
¾ cup sugar
1¾ cups ground walnuts
¼ cup semisweet chocolate pieces
3 tablespoons strong hot coffee
2 tablespoons seedless raspberry jam

Frosting

¼ cup unsalted butter, softened
¾ cup sifted confectioners' sugar
¼ cup semisweet chocolate pieces
3 tablespoons strong hot coffee
1 teaspoon vanilla

1. Preheat oven to 350°F. Using vegetable cooking spray, coat the bottom and sides of a 10-inch round cake pan with a removable bottom. Dust with about 1 teaspoon of flour.

2. Beat egg whites in a medium-size bowl until soft peaks form. In a large bowl beat 5 of the egg yolks with the sugar until thick, lemony colored, and light. Add half of the ground walnuts. Discard the extra yolk.

3. Melt the chocolate bits in the hot coffee and add slowly to the egg yolk mixture. Stir in a few tablespoons of the egg whites and mix well. Gently fold in remaining egg whites and walnuts.

4. Spoon cake batter into pan and bake for 1 hour, or until a cake tester comes out clean. Remove from pan and cool on wire rack. While cake is cooling make the frosting.

5. Beat the butter and sugar together until smooth and fluffy. Melt the chocolate bits in the hot coffee and add to the butter mixture, along with the vanilla. Mix well.

6. When the cake is completely cool, slice horizontally into two layers with a long serrated knife. Place the bottom layer on a pretty cake plate; spread with raspberry jam. Top with a thin layer of frosting. Set the other layer on top and frost completely with remaining frosting. Store in the refrigerator.

Memorial Day with Neighbors

Where I grew up, in northern New Jersey, the summer began with a neighborhood gathering at a pool built by the fathers and sons of the neighborhood. Traditionally, the fathers concocted a wicked punch, the mothers prepared delicous salads and desserts, and each family barbecued their own hunk of meat. Children of all ages joined together to create a play for entertaining the adults.

In New England, Memorial Day is as likely to bring a frost as a warm summer day, but we have persevered despite the weather and created our own tradition of a Memorial Day potluck picnic with our children and neighbors. So now our children will remember the holiday parade, the speeches, and walking down the hill to games and a picnic of hamburgers and homemade ice cream along Hemlock Brook on West Main Street.

This weekend menu evokes memories of things past, with some new twists. It is a long weekend with many meals. Being organized helps immensely. *E.S.*

~~~~~~~~~~~

Saturday
Dinner
Lemon Catfish* • Baked Butter Beans*
Endive and Radish Salad with Raspberry Vinaigrette*
Luscious Oatmeal Cookies* • Purple Plums

Sunday
Brunch
Orange French Toast* made with Swiss Braided Bread*
Cut-up Watermelon, Honeydew, and Peaches
Tomato Juice • Coffee and Tea

Supper
Surprising Baked Potatoes with Assorted Toppings*
Leftover Beans • Tender Lettuce Salad • Fresh Fruit

Monday — Memorial Day
Breakfast
Cold Cereal with Fruit • Breakfast Bar
Picnic
Healthy Nachos* with Kate's Fresh Salsa*
Grilled Pocket Burgers* • Chopped Cucumber Salad*
Curried Red Lentil Salad* • Vanilla Frozen Yogurt with
Fresh Strawberries and Hot Bittersweet Sauce*

*recipe included

THINGS TO DO AHEAD

THE WEEKEND BEFORE

- Get out your picnic tableware and cloth
- Bake and freeze Swiss Braided Bread
- Bake and freeze Oatmeal Cookies
- Make Bittersweet Sauce and store in refrigerator

THURSDAY

- Prepare Baked Butter Beans and refrigerate

FRIDAY

- Prepare toppings for Surprising Baked Potatoes
- Prepare Red Lentil Salad (except for final items)
- Wash, spin, and store greens for Endive and Radish Salad

WEEKEND WORK PLAN

SATURDAY MORNING

- Cut up fruit for Sunday
- Thaw Cookies and Bread

SATURDAY EVENING

- Warm Butter Beans
- Prepare Endive and Radish Salad
- Cook Lemon Catfish
- Serve dinner
- Just before bed, set up coffee and juice area

SUNDAY MORNING

- Arrange brunch table
- Prepare French Toast

SUNDAY

- Do something fun outdoors!

SUNDAY EVENING

- Prepare and bake Potatoes
- Arrange Toppings
- Prepare Chopped Cucumber Salad
- Before bed, set up breakfast bar

MONDAY MORNING

- After breakfast, prepare Pocket Burgers and chill
- Go to a parade!

MONDAY AFTERNOON

- Prepare Nachos and Kate's Salsa
- Prepare Cucumber Salad
- Complete Lentil Salad
- Grill Burgers
- Arrange food on table
- Eat, play games, and enjoy the day!

SPECIALTY ITEMS NEEDED

- Catfish
- Red lentils

Lemon Catfish

Farm-raised catfish is a popular dish in the South — there is even an annual catfish festival in Belzoni, Mississippi. For many in the rest of the United States, this mild and delicate fish is unknown at best, and considered a garbage fish at worst. One wonderful meal I was served in the South included crispy, deep-fried catfish and fried hush puppies. Catfish is also delectable cooked gently with subtle seasoning.

Preparation Time: 15 minutes • Serves 8

8 catfish fillets (about 2 pounds)
¼ cup lemon juice
2 tablespoons flour
¼ teaspoon salt
¼ teaspoon white pepper
1 teaspoon butter
1 teaspoon olive oil
¼ cup minced fresh parsley
1 lemon, cut in quarters

1. Rinse the fillets and pat dry. Pour the lemon juice into a flat baking dish and dip the fillets.
2. Mix the flour and seasonings together in a pie pan and turn the fillets in the flour mixture to coat.
3. In a large nonstick skillet melt the butter and oil over medium-high heat; quickly sauté the fish until the flesh is opaque and the outside lightly browned, about 2 minutes on each side.
4. Serve the catfish, sprinkled with parsley, on a platter with lemon wedges on the side.

Baked Butter Beans

Butter beans are baby lima beans. These ancient beans, named for the capital of Peru, date back thousands of years and have served as a dietary mainstay for many cultures. This version is definitely a make-ahead dish.

Preparation Time: 15 minutes • Baking Time: 1 hour • Serves 8

1 large onion, chopped
1 thin slice salt pork, or 1 slice bacon
1 small red hot pepper
4 cloves garlic, minced
Sprig of fresh thyme, or ½ teaspoon dried
4 cups fresh, shelled butter lima beans, or two 10-ounce packages frozen baby lima beans
1 teaspoon dry mustard
½ teaspoon salt
Freshly ground black pepper, to taste

1. In a large saucepan combine the onion, salt pork, pepper, garlic, and thyme with 3 cups of water and gently boil for 15–20 minutes. Remove the salt pork, pepper, and thyme.

2. Preheat oven to 325°F.

3. Pour the liquid into a 2-quart casserole dish; add the lima beans, mustard, salt, and pepper. Taste the liquid and correct the seasoning.

4. Bake for 1 hour, or until the beans are tender. Add more water if the beans lose their soupy quality. Serve warm or at room temperature.

Endive and Radish Salad with Raspberry Vinaigrette

Here is a quick, crunchy salad that can be put together at the last minute.

Preparation Time: 15 minutes • Serves 8

1 small head Romaine lettuce, washed and spun dry
1 small bunch arugula, washed and spun dry
2 bunches radishes, scrubbed, trimmed, and chopped
2 Belgian endives, cleaned and thinly sliced
1 small red onion, thinly sliced
3 oranges, peeled and cut into sections
2 tablespoons walnut oil
¼ cup raspberry vinegar
2 tablespoons crumbled feta cheese
Freshly ground white pepper, to taste

1. Prepare individual servings by arranging several lettuce leaves on each plate, followed by several sprigs of arugula.
2. Toss the radishes, endive, onions, and oranges together in a large bowl. Drizzle with the oil and toss. Sprinkle with the vinegar and toss again.
3. Spoon onto the prepared leaves; sprinkle with feta, season with a grating of pepper, and serve right away.

Luscious Oatmeal Cookies

Wonderful oatmeal cookies with a subtle spicy flavor.

Preparation Time: 20 minutes • Makes 2 dozen large cookies, or 4 dozen small ones

1½ cups all-purpose flour
½ cup whole wheat pastry flour
1 teaspoon ground cinnamon
1 teaspoon ground allspice
¼ teaspoon ground cloves
1 teaspoon ground ginger
½ teaspoon freshly ground black pepper
¼ teaspoon salt
½ teaspoon baking powder
¾ cup unsalted butter, softened
1 teaspoon vanilla
¾ cup sugar
¾ cup light brown sugar
1 egg
2 egg whites
3 cups rolled oats

1. Preheat oven to 375°F. Coat a baking sheet with vegetable cooking spray.
2. Sift the flours with spices, salt, and baking powder into a medium-size bowl.
3. In a large bowl beat the butter, vanilla, sugars, egg, and egg whites together until well blended. Gradually stir in the flour mixture until mixed well. Add the oats. Continue to stir until all the ingredients are well combined.
4. For large cookies drop ¼ cup dough for each cookie onto the baking sheet. For smaller cookies, use 1 tablespoon per cookie. Moisten fingers and flatten each cookie slightly.
5. Bake for 12–15 minutes or until the cookies are done in the middle and slightly browned. Remove from pan and cool on a rack.

Orange French Toast

Preparation Time: 30 minutes • Serves 6

1 loaf Swiss braided bread, cut into 12 slices
  (see following recipe)
4 eggs
4 egg whites
¼ teaspoon salt
1 tablespoon grated orange rind
½ cup orange juice

Orange Syrup
1½ cups orange juice
⅓ tablespoon sugar

1. In a large glass pie plate whisk together the eggs and egg whites. Add salt, orange rind, and orange juice; mix well.

2. Dip slices of bread in egg mixture and drain in another glass pie plate.

3. To make the orange syrup combine the orange juice and sugar in a small saucepan over medium heat. Bring to a boil and cook for 1 minute.

4. Heat a nonstick griddle or a large skillet brushed lightly with butter. Brown the bread; keep on a warm serving plate in a 200°F oven until ready to serve. Serve with the warm orange syrup.

Swiss Braided Bread

These beautiful braided loaves are delicious fresh, and the leftovers make excellent French toast. The loaves are also wonderful gifts. Make a double batch of this bread on a weekend when you have some extra time, and freeze several loaves for use when you don't have the time to bake it fresh.

Preparation Time: 30 minutes • Rising Time: 2 hours total • Baking Time: 40 minutes • Makes 2 large loaves

1 tablespoon active dry yeast
1 cup warm water
⅓ cup skim milk powder
2 tablespoons sugar
1 teaspoon salt
2 tablespoons butter
1 egg
3 cups flour, plus ½ cup if needed

Glaze
1 egg yolk beaten and mixed with 1 tablespoon water

1. In a large bowl sprinkle the yeast into the warm water; stir until dissolved. Add the milk powder, sugar, salt, butter, and egg; mix well to break the butter into small pieces.

2. Add 2 cups of the flour and beat the mixture with a wooden spoon until smooth. *Gradually* add the remaining 1 cup of flour and continue to stir with the wooden spoon. Remember it is easy to add more flour as needed, but impossible to remove flour if the dough becomes too stiff.

3. Scrape the dough out of the bowl and knead on a floured counter for 5–10 minutes until it is smooth and elastic. Add more flour if the dough becomes unmanageably sticky.

4. Plunk the smooth ball of dough into a large, lightly greased bowl; cover it with a damp towel and let it rise in a warm spot for 1 hour, or until double in bulk. Make a fist and punch down the dough. Divide the dough in two, with one half slightly bigger than the other. Divide the larger half into six equal pieces. Roll each piece into a 10 to 12-inch strand. Separate into two groups of three strands and make two braids. Repeat process with the smaller half to make two slightly smaller braids. Place the smaller braids on top of the larger ones to make two double-decked braided loaves. Coat a large baking sheet with vegetable cooking spray; arrange the loaves on the sheet, at least 6 inches apart. Cover with a towel and let the dough rise for about 1 hour.

5. Preheat oven to 400°F. Brush each loaf with the glaze. Bake the loaves for 40–50 minutes, or until lightly browned. Remove from the pan immediately and cool on a wire rack.

Surprising Baked Potatoes with Assorted Toppings

Here the lowly spud is taken to new heights, with surprises inside and decorations outside. For people who can't decide how they want their potato, they can have it all with this recipe.

Preparation Time: 15 minutes • Baking Time: 1 hour • Serves 8

8 large baking potatoes, washed and scrubbed
½–¾ cup herbed goat cheese
Olive oil
Coarse salt

TOPPINGS

- Salsa (see recipe on page 96)
- Mixture of half plain nonfat yogurt and half light sour cream
- Chopped steamed broccoli
- Freshly grated Parmesan cheese
- Chopped fresh herbs of your choice: chives, dill, basil, cilantro
- Low-fat cottage cheese or ricotta cheese

1. Preheat oven to 400°F.
2. With an apple corer, remove a plug from the center of half of the potatoes, boring in from both ends. Save the pieces. Pack a tablespoon of goat cheese into each cavity and plug each end with a reserved potato piece.
3. Brush all the potatoes with oil; sprinkle with a small amount of salt and bake for 1 hour, or until tender when pierced with a fork.
4. Serve hot with assorted toppings.

Healthy Nachos

Nachos are a favorite snack that are easy to make, and the variations are endless. Use your imagination to create your own version. You could use store-bought tortilla chips for nachos, but these baked chips are low in fat, taste delicious, and are simple to make. Put the young teenagers to work on these.

Preparation Time: 30 minutes • Makes appetizers for 8; lunch for 6

12 corn tortillas (the thinner the better)
2 teaspoons butter, softened
1 cup grated low-fat Monterey Jack cheese
   (or other cheese that melts well)
½ cup refried beans (optional), or cooked black beans

TOPPINGS
- 1½ cups Kate's Fresh Salsa
  (See following recipe. If you're
  in a rush use bottled, but fresh
  is best.)
- ½ cup plain nonfat yogurt
- Sliced jalapeño peppers

Optional:
- Chopped green onions
- Chopped green peppers

To make baked corn chips:
1. Preheat oven to 350°F.
2. Brush each tortilla with a very small amount of butter, and cut into 8 pie-shaped wedges using kitchen shears. Arrange wedges in a single layer on a cookie sheet; bake for about 10 minutes until crisp and slightly brown. Extras may be stored in an airtight container. The chips can be made in advance, cooled, and stored for several days.

To complete the nachos:
1. Spread some of the chips in a 10-inch deep-dish pie plate. Dab each with refried beans. Sprinkle cheese over the top. Microwave for 30 seconds on high.
2. Top with any combination of the toppings.

Tip for appetizer: Make a nacho plate with beans, and one without. Put the toppings in small bowls, give each person a small plate, and let people build their own nachos.

Kate's Fresh Salsa

Fresh salsa is best when tomatoes are in season. This recipe can be used in many Mexican dishes.

Preparation Time: 15 minutes • Makes 2 cups

2 large tomatoes, chopped and seeded
1 medium Vidalia or sweet onion, chopped
2 tablespoons lime juice (2 limes)
⅓ cup chopped fresh cilantro
2 tablespoons chopped green chiles
2 drops Tabasco sauce
Salt and freshly grated pepper, to taste

1. Mix all ingredients in a medium-size bowl. Let stand for 30 minutes to blend the flavors.
2. If you make the salsa ahead of time, leave out the chiles and add just before serving.

Grilled Pocket Burgers

Wendy, a hometown friend and wonderful cook and caterer, first prepared these at a picnic on Angel Island in San Francisco Bay years ago. They are a lovely change from plain old burgers.

Preparation Time: 20 minutes • Chilling Time: 3 hours • Serves 8

2 pounds lean ground lamb
1 egg white
½ cup fine fresh whole wheat bread crumbs
½ pound feta cheese, crumbled
4 cloves garlic, minced
2 teaspoons dried oregano
1 tablespoon ground cumin
¼ cup chopped fresh cilantro
¼ cup chopped fresh mint
8 pita pockets (whole wheat or plain)
2 medium tomatoes, sliced
1 small sweet onion, thinly sliced

1. In a large bowl combine the lamb, egg white, bread crumbs, half of the feta, and all the flavorings. Mix well with your hands; form into 8–12 patties, depending on the appetites in your group.
2. Refrigerate for at least 3 hours.
3. Preheat grill. Grill the lamb burgers until they are slightly pink inside, about 10 minutes on each side.
4. Cut the top third from each pita and insert the extra bread inside the pocket. Warm the pitas on the grill; slide the meat into the hot pockets. Serve with the remaining feta, tomatoes, onions, and chopped cucumber salad.

Chopped Cucumber Salad

A cool cucumber salad with refreshing yogurt is the perfect complement to a spicy main course. Indians serve raita to counterbalance a hot curry, and this salad does the same for the pita burgers and red lentils.

Preparation Time: 15 minutes • Makes 1½ cups

2 cucumbers, peeled and cut into ¼-inch chunks
1 cup plain nonfat yogurt
1 tablespoon chopped mint leaves
1 tablespoon chopped cilantro leaves
½ teaspoon ground cumin

Mix all ingredients together just before serving. Pour into a nice small serving bowl.

Curried Red Lentil Salad

This is an all-time favorite salad. Curry is a blend of many spices, which in India are purchased separately in the market and ground together. Curry powder is an attempt to replicate the blend of flavors with a combination of ground spices. There is no such thing as a curry plant. If your spice rack cannot produce the variety needed for this recipe, you can substitute curry powder for some or all of the spices. Check the curry powder label first, however, to see what you are substituting. If you mix the suggested spices, you will be rewarded by a rich, spicy blend that complements the relatively bland taste of the lentils.

Preparation Time: 30 minutes • Setting Time: Overnight • Serves 8

1 pound dried red lentils
1 cup currants
⅓ cup capers
1 medium red onion, thinly sliced

Vinaigrette
½ cup tarragon wine vinegar
1 tablespoon sugar
½ teaspoon salt
1 teaspoon ground cumin
1 teaspoon dry mustard
½ teaspoon turmeric
½ teaspoon mace
½ teaspoon coriander
½ teaspoon cardamom
¼ teaspoon cayenne pepper
¼ teaspoon ground cloves
¼ teaspoon nutmeg
¼ teaspoon cinnamon
Freshly ground pepper (about 2 teaspoons)
¾ cup canola oil
Fresh lettuce leaves, for serving

1. Rinse and pick over the lentils. Bring 2 cups water to a boil, add the lentils, and cook until they are just tender, about 10 minutes. You don't want them mushy. Rinse and drain the cooked lentils.

2. While the lentils cook, make the vinaigrette. Combine all the vinaigrette ingredients except the oil; mix well. Slowly whisk in the oil, not to get a thick emulsion but to combine well. Set aside.

3. Combine the lentils and vinaigrette and allow to set for several hours or overnight.

4. Several hours before serving, add the currants, capers, and onions to the salad and let it marinate. Serve the salad on fresh lettuce leaves arranged on a large plate.

Vanilla Frozen Yogurt with Fresh Strawberries and Hot Bittersweet Sauce

I can't get through strawberry season without combining luscious local berries with chocolate. This sauce has been a family favorite for years, and the original version is by no means low-fat. Lately I've been making batches that are almost as good and much kinder to the arteries — the lower fat substitutions are noted in the ingredient list.

Preparation Time: 30 minutes • Serves 8

1½ quarts fresh strawberries
½ gallon of your favorite vanilla frozen yogurt or light ice cream
1 batch of hot bittersweet sauce (see following recipe)

1. Just before serving, rinse the strawberries and remove the tops. Cut the berries in half but reserve 8 large perfect berries. (Good job for a helper.)
2. Warm up the sauce.
3. Ask another helper to dish the frozen yogurt into pretty glass dessert bowls. Spoon the strawberries over it and top with hot bittersweet sauce. Top each dish with a perfect berry and serve with a well-deserved flourish.

TIPS FOR STORING STRAWBERRIES:

- Don't remove stems
- Don't wash
- Don't store in refrigerator (except if for a long period)
- Rinse and hull berries just before using

Hot Bittersweet Sauce

This sauce can be made ahead and stored in a glass jar in the refrigerator. Reheat in a microwave, or place jar in a pan of gently boiling water until sauce softens.

Preparation Time: 15 minutes • Makes 1 cup

2 ounces unsweetened chocolate (*For lower fat:* substitute 6 tablespoons unsweetened cocoa powder and 2 tablespoons canola oil)
1 tablespoon butter (*For lower fat:* substitute 1 teaspoon butter)
⅓ cup boiling water
1 cup sugar
2 tablespoons light corn syrup
1 teaspoon vanilla

1. Combine the chocolate and butter (or the cocoa, oil, and butter) over low heat in a small saucepan; stir until melted and the mixture is well blended.
2. Add boiling water and stir well. Add sugar and corn syrup; bring to a boil. Let bubble gently over low heat for about 5 minutes without stirring. (Stirring causes sugar to crystallize, giving a grainy rather than a smooth sauce.) Be careful it doesn't burn. Add vanilla and remove from heat immediately.

A Celebration of High School Graduation

With teens around, eating can be constant. The plan for this weekend is to provide two meals a day that appeal to all ages and allow for some flexibility. Breakfast may be lunch, and lunch may be breakfast, when you've got a houseful of teens. A nice family meal prior to the ceremony is a worthy goal, and a gathering of friends and family after graduation is always fun. *E.S.*

Saturday
Lunch

Sandwich Bar with Sliced Turkey, Avocado, Red Onions,
Tomato, and Fontina Cheese
Radish Sprouts
Rye Bread, Multigrain Bread, Assorted Bagels
Red and Green Grapes

Dinner for Family from Afar

Lime Grilled Halibut*
Potato Gratin*
Green Garden Salad
Strawberry Rhubarb Crunch*

Sunday
Breakfast/Brunch

Leftover Crunch (from Saturday dinner)
Eggs, as you like them • Chilled Cantaloupe
Coffee/Tea

Late Afternoon Buffet Party for the Graduate, Family, and Friends

(following the ceremony)
Cold Cut Board with Assorted Crackers and Mustards
Grilled and Chilled Orange Chicken*
Spinach Pasta Roll with Creamy Tomato Sauce*
Colorful Coleslaw* • Barley Salad* • Garden Salad
Peppermint Punch* • Flavored Seltzer Waters
Cake (with appropriate decoration) • Light Lemon Bars*
Coffee and Tea

recipe included

THINGS TO DO AHEAD

THE WEEKEND BEFORE

- Get out tablecloths and party dishes
- Make Light Lemon Bars and freeze
- Assemble Spinach Pasta Roll and freeze
- Cook and freeze barley for salad

THURSDAY

- Prepare marinade for Orange Chicken
- Prepare marinade for Halibut
- Wash, spin, and store salad greens

FRIDAY

- Make Coleslaw dressing
- Shred cabbage for Coleslaw and store in zip-seal bag in refrigerator
- Make and chill Peppermint Punch
- Prepare Strawberry Rhubarb Crunch
- Make Creamy Tomato Sauce for Pasta Roll
- Prepare vegetables for Barley Salad and store in zip-seal bag in refrigerator

SPECIALTY ITEMS NEEDED:

- Sheets of fresh pasta

WEEKEND WORK PLAN

SATURDAY MORNING

- Marinate Orange Chicken
- Buy flowers
- Thaw barley and Pasta Roll
- Prepare Sandwich Bar so it is ready as people arrive
- Cook and slice potatoes for Gratin

SATURDAY EVENING

- Complete and cook Potatoes Gratin
- Grill Halibut and Orange Chicken; chill chicken
- Prepare green salad
- After dinner, warm Strawberry Rhubarb Crunch at a low oven temperature
- Just before bed, prepare coffee and juice area

SUNDAY MORNING

- Arrange brunch food before leaving for graduation
- Cook eggs, or let people cook their own
- Complete Colorful Coleslaw and Barley Salad; store in serving dishes in refrigerator
- Arrange dessert and coffee table for afternoon party

SUNDAY AFTERNOON (AFTER GRADUATION)

- Bake Spinach Pasta Roll
- Warm Creamy Tomato Sauce
- Slice Pasta Roll and arrange on platter with Tomato Sauce
- Enjoy the party!

Lime Grilled Halibut

Halibut is a nice, firm-fleshed fish that grills well. It has a lot of fat under the skin which can cause the grill to flare up, so have some water on hand. Use a fish basket if you have one, otherwise use large spatulas for turning the fish.

Preparation Time: 15 minutes • Marinating Time: 45 minutes • Cooking Time: 15 minutes • Serves 6

2½ pounds halibut steaks
2 limes, cut in wedges
Basil leaves

Marinade
½ cup lime juice
¼ cup olive oil
¼ cup soy sauce
2 cloves garlic, mashed
¼ cup fresh chopped basil
Freshly ground pepper

1. Rinse and dry the fish steaks; lay in a shallow nonmetallic dish.
2. Mix the marinade ingredients and pour over the steaks. Cover with plastic wrap and let sit in refrigerator for 30 minutes.
3. Prepare the grill; remove fish from the refrigerator.
4. When the fire is hot, grill the fish for 5–10 minutes on each side (depending on thickness), or until the flesh is opaque. Arrange the fish on a platter; garnish with basil leaves and lime wedges.

Potato Gratin

Preparation Time: 30 minutes • Baking Time: 1 hour • Serves 6

8 cups thinly sliced unpeeled red potatoes
   (about 6 large potatoes)
¼ cup all-purpose flour
½ cup finely chopped Italian parsley
1 large onion, thinly sliced
½ teaspoon salt
1 teaspoon butter
2 cups evaporated skimmed milk
Freshly ground pepper to taste

1. Preheat oven to 350°F. Pat the potatoes dry with paper towels. Toss them in a large bowl with flour, basil, parsley, and onion slices until the potatoes and onions are coated with flour and the herbs are distributed throughout.

2. Arrange the potatoes in a large shallow baking dish that has been lightly coated with vegetable cooking spray. Season with salt and pepper and dot with butter. Pour the milk over the potatoes until it just covers them but does not rise above. Cover the pan with foil and bake for 1 hour, or until the potatoes are tender.

Strawberry Rhubarb Crunch

A wonderful version of this favorite combination of flavors! I make this delicious dish over and over again until the rhubarb is all gone. The combination of custard sauce and the crunch is heavenly. An alternative is to serve it with vanilla frozen yogurt, or vanilla nonfat yogurt.

Preparation Time: 30 minutes • Baking Time: 45 minutes • Serves 8

Custard Sauce

2 eggs
⅓ cup sugar
2 cups skim milk
¼ teaspoon salt
1 split vanilla bean

Filling

2 cups fresh strawberries, cut in half
4 cups fresh rhubarb, cut into 1-inch pieces
1½ cups honey
½ teaspoon ground cinnamon
1 orange, peeled and cut in sections with membrane removed

Topping

½ cup whole wheat pastry flour
¾ cup rolled oats
½ cup brown sugar
4 tablespoons butter
1 tablespoon canola oil
¼ cup chopped pecans, toasted
1 teaspoon grated orange rind

1. To make the custard sauce, beat the eggs and sugar together in a heavy saucepan.
2. In another saucepan, heat the milk, salt, and vanilla bean until almost simmering. Slowly add the hot milk to the eggs, stirring constantly.
3. Cook until mixture thickens and coats a wooden spoon; strain, and chill in a glass jar in the refrigerator.
4. Preheat oven to 375°F. Coat a 2-quart casserole with vegetable cooking spray.
5. Toss the strawberries, rhubarb, honey, cinnamon, and orange together in a large bowl and pour into the casserole.
6. In a small bowl make the topping by mixing the flour, oats, and brown sugar together with a fork. With a pastry blender cut the butter and oil into the mixture until it is crumbly. Stir in the pecans and orange rind.
7. Sprinkle topping over strawberry rhubarb mixture and bake for 35–40 minutes until filling is bubbly and topping is nicely browned. Cool on wire rack.
8. Serve warm with cold custard sauce or yogurt.

Grilled and Chilled Orange Chicken

Chicken thighs are wonderful for a buffet because they are relatively small, have a nice serving of meat on their bones, and come in quite uniform sizes.

Preparation Time: 30 minutes • Marinating Time: Overnight
Cooking Time: 20–30 minutes • Chilling Time: 2 hours • Serves 8

4 pounds chicken thighs (12 pieces), skin removed

Marinade
2 tablespoons grated orange rind
Juice of 3 oranges (about 1 cup)
½ teaspoon ground cumin
3 cloves garlic, mashed
¼ cup chopped fresh cilantro
2 tablespoons chopped fresh mint
2 tablespoons sesame oil
¼ cup rice vinegar

Garnish
1 orange, thinly sliced
Sprigs of cilantro

1. Rinse and pat dry the chicken and arrange in a shallow baking dish. Whisk together the marinade ingredients and pour over the chicken. Cover and refrigerate overnight.

2. Prepare the grill. Remove the chicken from the marinade and discard the marinade. Cook the chicken over a low fire on a gas grill, or on a high rack on a charcoal grill, for 20–30 minutes until the outsides are golden brown and the insides are cooked through, turning several times.

3. Arrange the chicken on a platter, garnish with the orange and cilantro, cover with plastic wrap, and chill until the party. This chicken is delicious served hot as well.

Spinach Pasta Roll with Creamy Tomato Sauce

This dish requires a large sheet of fresh pasta. If you make your own, you are all set; if not, find a market that makes fresh pasta. I have to drive 45 minutes to such a market, so I usually stock up on sheets of fresh pasta and freeze them well wrapped. They're wonderful for lasagna. You may need to make more than one roll depending on how many people you're hosting. The pasta roll can be made ahead and reheated, or it can be frozen uncooked and then cooked just before serving.

Preparation Time: 1 hour • Baking Time: 45 minutes • Makes 2 rolls (each serves 8)

Filling

2 pounds fresh spinach, washed (with water still on it), or
    two 10-ounce packages of frozen spinach, thawed
1 medium onion, minced
1 teaspoon olive oil
2 cups part-skim milk ricotta cheese
1 egg and 1 egg white, slightly beaten
1 cup freshly grated Parmesan cheese
½ teaspoon salt
¼ teaspoon freshly ground pepper
A dash of cayenne pepper
¼ teaspoon nutmeg
¼ pound thinly sliced prosciutto, sliced, with much of the fat
    removed
Two 10 by 14-inch sheets of fresh pasta

Creamy Tomato Sauce

3 tablespoons minced shallots
1 tablespoon olive oil
4 large good-quality tomatoes, peeled and chopped, with
    juice and seeds reserved
½ teaspoon salt

A dash of cayenne pepper
1 tablespoon minced fresh basil
1 tablespoon butter
1 tablespoon flour
1 cup skim milk
Extra Parmesan cheese for serving

1. To make the filling, cook the spinach in a large kettle until it is wilted and the liquid is evaporated. Chop and set aside.

2. In a large skillet cook the onion in the oil for about 5 minutes until golden. Add the spinach and continue cooking until all liquid is evaporated.

3. Combine the spinach with ricotta, egg and egg white, Parmesan, salt, peppers, and nutmeg in a large bowl; mix well.

4. In a skillet over medium heat cook the prosciutto for several minutes; add it to the spinach mixture, mix well, and set aside.

5. Preheat oven to 350°F.

6. Slip one uncooked sheet of fresh pasta into a roasting pan of boiling water. Pour off the hot water, and add cold water. Remove the pasta from pan and lay on a clean surface. Spread half the filling evenly on the pasta and roll it up lengthwise. Repeat with the other sheet. Dry the roasting pan and coat it with olive oil cooking spray.

7. Carefully place the pasta rolls, seam side down, in the roasting pan. Rub 1 teaspoon olive oil over the rolls, and bake for 30–45 minutes, or until the filling is set. Let sit for 10 minutes before slicing.

8. Cut the rolls into 1-inch slices; arrange on a platter and serve warm with creamy tomato sauce and Parmesan cheese.

9. While the pasta rolls are cooking, make the creamy tomato sauce. In a small saucepan cook the shallots in the olive oil over medium heat until they are tender but not browned, 5–7 minutes. Strain the reserved tomato juice and seeds into the mixture and cook until very thick, stirring constantly for about 5 minutes.

10. Add the tomatoes, salt, and cayenne and continue cooking until all the liquid has evaporated and you have a thick, concentrated sauce. Add the basil and cool.

11. Complete the sauce by melting the butter in a small saucepan over low heat. Add flour and cook for 1 minute. Add milk, increase heat to medium, and cook until mixture boils and thickens. Add the sauce to the tomato mixture. Heat gently and serve with hot pasta roll sprinkled on top with Parmesan.

~~~~~~~~~~

Colorful Coleslaw

Preparation Time: 15 minutes • *Serves 8*

½ small head red cabbage, finely shredded (about 3 cups)
3 large carrots, peeled and grated
2 tablespoons minced fresh dill

Dressing
1 cup evaporated skimmed milk
2 tablespoons cider vinegar
2 tablespoons sugar
¼ teaspoon salt
¼ cup plain nonfat yogurt

1. Combine the cabbage, carrots, and dill in a large bowl and toss to mix.
2. To make the dressing, combine the milk and vinegar in a small bowl and let it stand for a few minutes until the milk sours and thickens slightly. Add the sugar, salt, and yogurt; gently stir until just combined.
3. Put the coleslaw in a serving bowl, pour the dressing over it, and toss.

~~~~~~~~~~

Barley Salad

Preparation Time: 20 minutes • *Serves 8*

2½ cups of chicken stock
1¼ cups barley
2 tablespoons chopped sun-dried tomatoes
2 large ripe tomatoes, chopped and seeded (optional)
3 green onions, minced, using both white and green part
½ cup minced parsley
¾ cup mixed chopped red, yellow and green peppers
¼ cup good quality, extra virgin olive oil
⅓ cup red wine vinegar
Salt and freshly ground black pepper, to taste
2 tablespoons crumbled feta cheese

1. Bring the chicken stock to a boil in a large saucepan. Add the barley, cover the pot, and cook over low heat for 30 minutes until the grain has puffed and absorbed the liquid.
2. Fluff with a fork and cool slightly. Add the remaining ingredients and toss well to mix. Serve the salad at room temperature in an attractive bowl.

Light Lemon Bars

This lower fat version of a delicious two-layer bar cookie is a favorite of teenagers.

Preparation Time: 20 minutes • Baking Time: 40 minutes altogether • Makes 12 squares

Crust
3 tablespoons sugar
¾ cup flour
¼ cup butter

Topping
2 slightly beaten egg whites
1 beaten egg
¾ cup sugar
½ teaspoon finely shredded lemon peel
3 tablespoons lemon juice
2 tablespoons flour
¼ teaspoon baking powder
Confectioners' sugar, for garnish

1. Preheat oven to 350°F and coat an 8 by 8 by 2-inch baking pan with vegetable cooking spray.
2. To make the crust, combine sugar and flour in a medium-size bowl. Cut in the butter with a pastry blender or your fingers until the mixture resembles coarse crumbs. Pat into the pan and bake for 15 minutes, until lightly browned.
3. Meanwhile make the topping by whisking together the egg whites and egg. Add sugar, lemon peel, lemon juice, flour, and baking powder. Continue beating with a whisk until slightly thickened.
4. Pour the lemon mixture over the crust and bake for another 25 minutes. Cool and sift confectioners' sugar over top. Cut into bars.

Peppermint Punch

Preparation Time: 15 minutes • Chilling Time: 45 minutes • Makes 3 quarts

6 bags peppermint tea
2 quarts boiling water
1 tablespoon honey
1 quart cranberry juice cocktail
Juice of 1 lime
Sprigs of mint

1. Place tea bags in a heavy glass pitcher, add the boiling water and the honey and let the mixture steep for 30 minutes.
2. Remove tea bags, add cranberry and lime juices, and chill. Serve in tall glasses over ice, garnished with a sprig of mint.

Summer is the season to be outdoors, eat outdoors, work and play outdoors. In New England it gets warm and occasionally hot, but seldom is it hazy, hot, and humid for long periods. Gardens grow; fresh fruits, berries, and produce fill the markets; and eating the season's bounty is sheer delight. From strawberries to raspberries to blueberries to blackberries, the meadows and fields yield an incredible bounty of delicious, fresh, healthy fruits and vegetables.

Perhaps this serene summer weather is our reward for putting up with long, cold winters. Cooking becomes very simple in the summer because some of the best meals consist of food fresh from the garden or farm stand. There is nothing to beat a ripe tomato warm from the sun, served with a fresh basil leaf and drizzled with olive oil, except perhaps a strawberry at its prime eaten in the field. Summer is the food lover's delight. The days are long, the pace is slow, dining is casual, and eating is at its best.

Weekend on the Boat

I fantasize about boating weekends, and have actually been on a few. The best was on a day sailer in the Virgin Islands where someone else took care of the sailing and the food. My boating experience consists mostly of canoeing across northern lakes in search of loons, and picnicking on beautiful little islands. This menu is designed for eating on land — definitely not in a canoe — with the exception of Saturday lunch and Sunday brunch. Ask your guests to bring the appetizers for Saturday dinner. Bring plenty of food because being on the water all day brings out appetites, even of those lolling on the deck. *E.S.*

Friday
Supper

Summer Spaghetti*
Garden Green Salad
Awesome Blueberry Pie*

Saturday
Basic Breakfast Bar

(see page 3)

Lunch on the Boat

Tomato Basil Sandwiches*
Fresh Peaches • Super Chip Cookies*
Chilled Mineral Water and Sparkling Juices

Dinner

Potluck Appetizers
Lemon Chicken and Vegetable Kebabs*
Grilled Corn*
Nectarine Blueberry Crisp*
Fresh Lemonade*

Sunday
Brunch on the Boat

Leftover Nectarine Blueberry Crisp
Veggie Strata*
Chilled Melon
Juices, Coffee, and Tea

recipe included

THINGS TO DO AHEAD

THE WEEKEND BEFORE

- Prepare and freeze crust for Blueberry Pie
- Bake and freeze Super Chip Cookies
- Make sugar syrup for Lemonade
- Organize the picnic basket, utensils, glasses, plates, and food containers you will need on the boat

THURSDAY

- Make Blueberry Pie
- Make Nectarine Blueberry Crisp

FRIDAY

- Prepare marinade for Lemon Chicken and Vegetable Kebabs
- Cut up Vegetables for Kebabs and store in zip-seal bag

SPECIALTY ITEMS NEEDED

- Metal or bamboo skewers

WEEKEND WORK PLAN

FRIDAY EVENING

- Thaw Cookies
- Cook pasta and prepare sauce for Summer Spaghetti
- Make green salad
- Just before bed, prepare Basic Breakfast Bar set-up

SATURDAY MORNING

- Complete breakfast bar preparations
- Eat!
- Prepare Tomato Basil Sandwiches
- Pack up boat food; go out and have a great day on the water

SATURDAY EVENING

- Marinate the Chicken and Vegetables for Kebabs as soon as you get home
- Soak corn
- Arrange appetizers and set table
- Grill Lemon Chicken and Vegetable Kebabs and corn
- Just before bed, prepare Veggie Strata and coffee and juice area

SUNDAY MORNING

- Bake Strata; wrap in towel and take to boat
- Pack up remaining brunch food

Summer Spaghetti

When the tomatoes are ripe and the weather is hot, you will love this fresh-tasting spaghetti dinner.

Preparation Time: 30 minutes • Serves 6

1 pound spaghetti
Olive oil (enough to coat the pasta)
⅓ pound part-skim milk mozzarella or other cheese, cut into ¼-inch cubes
6–8 black olives, cut in half
1 clove garlic, minced
3 fresh ripe tomatoes, cut into bite-size chunks
A handful of fresh basil leaves, chopped
2 tablespoons minced fresh parsley
A dash of red pepper
½ teaspoon dried oregano
Salt and freshly ground pepper, to taste

1. In a large kettle of boiling salted water cook the pasta until al dente. Drain and toss with olive oil.

2. Meanwhile, prepare the sauce in large serving bowl by combining the remaining ingredients.

3. When the pasta is done, pour it on top of the sauce and let it sit for a few minutes. Toss and serve immediately.

Awesome Blueberry Pie

Many blueberries grace this wonderfully fresh-tasting pie that can be made quickly.

Preparation Time: 20 minutes • Makes one 10-inch pie

One 10-inch pie shell, baked (use pie dough found in the refrigerated section of the supermarket or your favorite recipe)
2 quarts blueberries
½ cup sugar
½ cup brown sugar
¼ teaspoon cinnamon
¼ teaspoon salt
1 teaspoon butter
2 tablespoons cornstarch
2 tablespoons lemon juice

1. In a large heavy saucepan mix together 1 quart of the blueberries, the sugars, cinnamon, salt, and butter and mash slightly. Dissolve the cornstarch in the lemon juice and add to the mixture. Cook over medium heat until the mixture bubbles and thickens. Cook for 5 minutes longer, stirring frequently.

2. Cool the blueberry mixture and add the remaining uncooked blueberries. Fill the pie shell and chill. Serve plain or with vanilla frozen yogurt.

Tomato Basil Sandwiches

An all-time great summer sandwich!

Preparation Time: 15 minutes • Makes 6 sandwiches

Version 1

Loaf of your favorite whole grain soft bread
One 8-ounce package light cream cheese
  (you will not use all of it)
3 fresh medium-size tomatoes, thinly sliced
Salt and freshly ground pepper, to taste
A handful of fresh basil leaves

1. Spread a thin layer of cream cheese on 6 slices of bread.
2. Arrange tomato slices on top of the cheese and season with salt and pepper.
3. Cover tomatoes with basil leaves; top each with another slice of bread. Cut into halves and serve.

Version 2

Italian semolina bread, sliced
3 fresh medium-size tomatoes, thinly sliced
Salt and freshly ground pepper, to taste
A handful of fresh basil leaves
Good quality extra-virgin olive oil

1. Arrange tomato slices on top of 6 slices of bread; season with salt and pepper.
2. Cover tomatoes with basil leaves, sprinkle with olive oil, and top each with second slice of bread. Cut into halves and serve.

Super Chip Cookies

Preparation Time: 30 minutes • Baking Time: 10 minutes • Makes 3 dozen large cookies

¾ cup unsalted butter
¾ cup granulated sugar
¾ cup brown sugar
1 egg
2 egg whites
1 teaspoon vanilla
1½ cups all-purpose flour
½ cup whole wheat pastry flour
½ teaspoon salt
1 teaspoon baking powder
1 teaspoon baking soda
2½ cups rolled oats
1½ cups bittersweet chocolate chips (semi-sweet chips can be substituted, but bittersweet are preferable)
One 4-ounce chocolate bar, grated
⅓ cup chopped walnuts

1. Preheat oven to 375°F.
2. In the large bowl of an electric mixer beat butter and sugars until creamy. Add the egg, egg whites, and vanilla and beat until light and fluffy.
3. Sift the dry ingredients into the bowl, add oats, and beat at low speed until well mixed. Add the chocolates and nuts and mix well with a wooden spoon.
4. Drop by large spoonfuls onto an ungreased baking sheet about 2 inches apart; bake for 10–12 minutes, or until lightly browned on edges. Cookies will be soft in center until they cool. Freeze or store in an airtight container.

Lemon Chicken and Vegetable Kebabs

Preparation Time: 20 minutes • Marinating Time: 1–2 hours • Cooking Time: 30 minutes • Serves 8

10–16 skewers
3 whole chicken breasts, boned, skinned, and cut into
   1-inch chunks
3 small zucchini cut into ½-inch slices
2 cups cherry tomatoes
2 Vidalia onions, cut into thick slices
½ pound white mushrooms, cut in half
Any vegetables that appeal to you

Marinade

¼ cup canola oil
½ cup lemon juice
½ teaspoon salt
2 teaspoons dried marjoram
2 teaspoons thyme
1 teaspoon freshly ground black pepper
2–3 cloves garlic, minced
1 small onion, chopped
½ cup chopped fresh parsley

Note: If you use bamboo skewers, soak them in cold
water for at least 1 hour before grilling.

1. Mix all the marinade ingredients together. Put the chicken chunks in a medium-size bowl and pour three-quarters of the marinade over them. Stir enough to coat all the pieces.

2. Pour the rest of the marinade over the vegetables and gently mix in a large bowl. Cover the chicken and the vegetables and store in the refrigerator for 1 to 2 hours.

3. Thirty minutes before grilling, prepare the grill. Thread the chicken onto skewers, leaving about ¼-inch space between each chunk. Arrange the vegetables in a colorful manner on skewers. Save the veggie marinade to use on leftovers; throw away the chicken marinade.

4. Carefully lay the chicken skewers on the hot grill. Cook for about 5 minutes; turn and cook another 5 minutes, or until the chicken is firm to the touch.

5. Add the vegetable skewers to the grill once the chicken is done. Cook the veggies for 5 minutes, or until they begin to brown and soften. But don't let them get mushy.

6. If you have any leftover veggies, put them back in the marinade; store in the refrigerator and serve as a salad.

Grilled Corn

Boiled fresh corn is great, but grilling gives it a slightly smokey flavor.

Preparation Time: 15 minutes • Soaking Time: 1 hour • Serves 6

One dozen ears of fresh corn

1. Pull back husks, remove silk, and replace husks on corn. Soak corn in a large kettle of water for an hour.
2. Preheat grill.
3. Grill corn for about 10 minutes until the husks become browned on all sides.
4. Remove corn from grill, husk it, and serve with your favorite seasonings.

Fresh Lemonade

An excellent way to get through a heat wave! I keep a jar of sugar syrup in the refrigerator in steamy weather so I can make up a glass of fresh lemonade quickly.

Preparation Time: 15 minutes • Makes 6–8 glasses

Sugar Syrup
2 cups sugar
Rind of 2 lemons, cut in strips
1 cup water

Lemonade
Juice of 8 lemons (1 cup lemon juice)
Mint leaves

1. Cook sugar, lemon rind, and water in a heavy, medium-size saucepan over medium heat until the sugar dissolves, about 5 minutes. Remove rind and store the syrup in a covered jar, either in the refrigerator or the cupboard.
2. To make the lemonade, fill eight tall glasses with ice; pour in 1–2 tablespoons of syrup and 1–2 tablespoons of lemon juice. Fill each glass with water and garnish with a sprig of mint.

Nectarine Blueberry Crisp

Make two, so you have an extra one to serve for Sunday brunch.

Preparation Time: 20 minutes • Baking Time: 40–50 minutes • Serves 8

Fruit

2 large, juicy nectarines, cut into ½-inch wedges
3 cups blueberries, rinsed and drained
⅓ cup sugar
Dash of ground cloves
1 tablespoon instant tapioca

Topping

¾ cups rolled oats
⅓ cup brown sugar
½ cup all-purpose flour
1 teaspoon grated lemon rind
¼ cup unsalted butter

1. Preheat oven to 375°F.
2. Toss fruit with sugar, cloves, and tapioca in a large bowl; let stand while making the topping.
3. Combine the oats, sugar, flour, and lemon rind in a medium-size bowl. With a pastry blender cut in the butter until mixture resembles a coarse meal.
4. Pour fruit into a 2-quart casserole that has been coated with vegetable cooking spray. Scatter the topping over the fruit and bake for 40–50 minutes, or until the fruit is bubbly. Serve warm or at room temperature.

Veggie Strata

Preparation Time: 30 minutes • Setting Time: Overnight • Baking Time: 1 hour • Serves 6

8 large slices of Italian semolina bread or French bread
2 cups grated zucchini
2 sweet Italian sausages, browned, crumbled, and well drained to remove excess fat (use Italian turkey sausage if you can find tasty ones)
1 medium onion, chopped
2 cups grated sharp cheddar or Gruyère cheese (depends on your preference; both work well and taste wonderful)
4 eggs
2 egg whites
3 cups evaporated skimmed milk
1 teaspoon dried thyme
¼ teaspoon dry mustard
¼ teaspoon salt
¼ teaspoon white pepper
2 tablespoons freshly grated Parmesan cheese

1. Lightly coat a shallow 2-quart casserole dish with vegetable cooking spray and line with four slices of the bread. Scatter the zucchini and sausage over the bread; sprinkle with onions and cheese. Lay the remaining bread slices over the cheese.

2. In a large bowl whisk the eggs and egg whites together until foamy. Add the milk, thyme, mustard, salt, and pepper and mix well; pour mixture over the bread. Cover the casserole with plastic wrap and let sit in the refrigerator overnight.

3. Preheat oven to 350°F.

4. Sprinkle strata with Parmesan and bake for 45 minutes to 1 hour or until it is puffy and golden brown. Serve hot!

July 4th Weekend

Each July, my son-in-law Chip's family invites a crowd to celebrate Independence Day at their sprawling farm in New York State. Before he was married to Wendy, Chip's Michigan buddies came and barbecued beef, camped out, celebrated, and departed. Times have changed and the guest list has grown. The Harleys of the past have been replaced by station wagons toting playpens and mountain bikes, as well as nutrition-conscious moms and dads.

Feeding this bunch has become quite a challenge. One Fourth, after way too many hours of kitchen duty, Wendy and her mother-in-law, Carolyne, instituted meal teams. Now, before their arrival, each guest is assigned to a "meal team." Each team is responsible for planning, shopping, cooking, and clean-up for one meal. Balanced teams are the goal: experienced cooks are spread around and they happily assign chopping, set-up, and clean-up chores to their less-inclined teammates. A certain competitive spirit has developed, and a predeparture poll is taken to determine which team has most successfully met the needs of this demanding culinary audience. *P.W.*

Friday
Evening Supper
Citrus Grilled Tuna*
Ratatouille*
Warm Wild Rice Salad*
Fresh Peaches
Dodge Bars*

Saturday
Breakfast
Seasonal Fruit • Glorious Granola* • Low-fat Yogurt
Assorted Cold Cereals

Lunch
Roast Turkey Sandwiches
(with Brie slices, honey mustard, lettuce, and
tomatoes on kaiser rolls)
Peanut Butter and Green Apple Sandwiches (on wheat
bread, cut into star shapes)
Lemonade • Cranberry Sparklers*

Cookout
Saté Babi*
Creamy Crunchy Potato Bake*
Sliced Tomatoes with fresh chopped basil,
extra-virgin olive oil, and balsamic vinegar
Raspberry Sherbert and Vanilla Frozen Yogurt
with Blueberries

Sunday
Brunch
Grapefruit Juice
Overnight Oven French Toast* • Apple Sausage Bake*
Oranges cut into quarters and garnished with fresh mint
Hazelnut Coffee

recipe included

THINGS TO DO AHEAD

THE WEEKEND BEFORE

- Bake and freeze Dodge Bars
- Make Glorious Granola

WEDNESDAY

- Prepare Saté Babi marinade

THURSDAY

- Prepare Citrus Marinade for tuna
- Make Ratatouille and refrigerate
- Assemble Wild Rice Salad and refrigerate

FRIDAY

- Add tuna to Citrus Marinade; refrigerate, turning after 3 hours
- Boil and cube potatoes for Creamy Crunchy Potato Bake
- Prepare, but don't cook, Apple Sausage Bake; refrigerate
- Thaw Dodge Bars

WEEKEND WORK PLAN

FRIDAY EVENING

- Remove Ratatouille from refrigerator
- Arrange Dodge Bars on serving plate
- Slice lemons and limes for garnishing Grilled Tuna
- Heat grill
- Bake Wild Rice Salad

- Grill Tuna
- Add pork and onions to marinade for Saté Babi; refrigerate overnight
- Just before bed, set up coffee and juice area

SATURDAY MORNING

- Set up breakfast buffet

SATURDAY MIDDAY

- Prepare sandwiches for lunch

SATURDAY AFTERNOON

- Assemble Potato Bake
- Clean blueberries for dessert topping
- Prepare Overnight Oven French Toast and refrigerate
- Assemble Saté Babi

SATURDAY EVENING

- Heat grill
- Bake Potato Bake
- Prepare sliced tomatoes and basil
- Grill Saté Babi
- Just before bed, set up coffee and juice area

SUNDAY MORNING

- Set up breakfast area
- Cut oranges in quarters
- Bake Apple Sausage Bake
- Bake Overnight Oven French Toast

Citrus Grilled Tuna

This fresh marinade is wonderful for any grilled fish.

Preparation Time: 15 minutes • Marinating Time: 6 hours • Grilling Time: About 15 minutes • Serves 8

1 cup grapefruit juice
1 cup orange juice
¼ cup lime juice
½ cup light soy sauce
1 tablespoon fresh chopped thyme leaves, or 1
   teaspoon dried
¼ teaspoon cayenne pepper
3 pounds tuna steaks
Lemon and lime slices, for garnish

1. Whisk together the juices, soy sauce, thyme, and pepper. Place tuna steaks in a shallow baking dish. Pour marinade over fish and refrigerate for 6 hours, turning fish after 3 hours.
2. Preheat grill and lightly oil racks.
3. Remove tuna from marinade and place on grill. Turn after about 7 minutes and continue grilling until fish is opaque (about 7 more minutes).
4. Place fish on a heated platter and garnish with lemon and lime slices. Serve immediately.

Ratatouille

This opulent dish is easier to prepare than the classic recipe, which calls for sautéing some of the vegetables. It is best prepared a day in advance. Leftovers are delicious served with crumbled goat cheese in a pita pocket.

Preparation Time: 20 minutes plus 1 hour for draining eggplant • Cooking Time: 1 hour and 15 minutes • Serves 6–8

1 medium eggplant
Salt, for sprinkling
1 large onion, chopped
2 green peppers, seeded and thinly sliced
2 medium, or 4 small, zucchini, diced
6 medium tomatoes, seeded and diced
2 large cloves garlic, crushed
Salt and freshly ground pepper, to taste
1 tablespoon sugar
1 tablespoon red wine vinegar
1 tablespoon dried oregano
1 teaspoon dried marjoram
5 tablespoons extra-virgin olive oil
½ cup water
25 pitted black olives
¼ cup finely chopped fresh basil
¼ cup finely chopped fresh parsley

1. Cut the eggplant in half lengthwise. Slash the cut surface and sprinkle it with salt. Lay the eggplant, cut side down, on paper towels for 1 hour to drain out the bitter water. Cut into ½-inch cubes.

2. In a heavy kettle gently toss together all ingredients except the oil, water, olives, basil, and parsley. Add the olive oil and the water, cover, and cook slowly over low heat until tender, about 1 hour.

3. Remove cover and cook 10 minutes more to reduce liquid. Stir in olives, basil, and parsley and cook 5 more minutes. Remove from heat and let cool a bit. Serve warm or at room temperature.

Warm Wild Rice Salad

The touch of orange makes this salad a refreshing companion to anything cooked on the grill. It can be assembled ahead and baked the day of the party.

Preparation Time: 40 minutes • Baking Time: 30 minutes • Serves 6–8

5½ cups water
1 cup wild rice
1 cup long grain rice
½ cup pine nuts, toasted
¼ cup chopped fresh parsley
2 tablespoons grated orange rind
¼ cup extra-virgin olive oil
2 tablespoons orange juice
Salt and freshly ground pepper, to taste

1. Preheat oven to 350°F.
2. Bring 3 cups of water to a boil; stir in the wild rice. Reduce heat, cover, and simmer for 25 minutes. Drain.
3. Bring 2½ cups of water to a boil; stir in long grain rice. Reduce heat, cover, and simmer for 20 minutes. Drain.
4. Toss rices together in a large bowl. Add pine nuts, parsley, orange rind, olive oil, and juice; mix thoroughly and season to taste.
5. Place mixture in casserole and bake, covered, for 30 minutes. Serve warm or cold.

Dodge Bars

These delicious, rich raspberry and currant bars were inspired by a recipe created by American baker Jim Dodge.

Preparation Time: 30 minutes • Baking Time: 55 minutes total • Chilling Time: Overnight • Makes about 18 bars

Crust

12 tablespoons unsalted butter
¾ cup confectioners' sugar
2 cups cake flour
½ teaspoon salt

1. Preheat oven to 350°F.
2. In a medium-size mixing bowl blend butter and sugar until just smooth. Add flour and salt and mix until dough resembles large crumbs. Press dough evenly into the bottom of a 9 by 13-inch pan.
3. Bake for 15–20 minutes until lightly browned. Allow pan to cool on wire rack.

Topping

1 large egg (at room temperature)
2 egg whites
1 cup sugar
¼ cup unsalted butter, melted and cooled
¼ cup unsweetened applesauce
½ cup shredded unsweetened coconut
1 cup currants
1⅓ cups finely chopped pecans
3 tablespoons apple cider vinegar
⅓–½ cup seedless raspberry preserves

1. In a large bowl whisk together the egg, egg whites, and sugar until smooth; whisk in the melted butter.
2. Fold in the applesauce, coconut, currants, pecans, and vinegar; mix until combined.
3. Carefully spread the preserves over the top of the crust in a thin layer.
4. Spread the topping mixture evenly over the preserves. Bake for 30–35 minutes, or until the top is evenly browned.
5. Cool to room temperature on wire rack. Chill in refrigerator overnight before cutting into small bars. (Clearly, these are in the category of goodies to eat in small quantities.)

Glorious Granola

Granola is too high in calories and fat to be considered an everyday breakfast cereal; use it as a topping for fruit and yogurt. It also makes a great hostess gift when poured into an attractive large glass jar.

Preparation Time: 30 minutes • Cooking Time: About 45 minutes • Makes about 10 cups

6 cups rolled oats
1 cup wheat germ
1 cup skim milk powder
½ cup sliced almonds
½ cup chopped hazelnuts
½ cup shelled sunflower seeds
½ cup sesame seeds
2 teaspoons cinnamon
1 cup honey
1 cup canola oil
2 teaspoons vanilla
¾ cup golden raisins
¾ cup dark raisins
½ cup dried cherries
½ cup dried cranberries

1. Preheat oven to 325°F.
2. In a large bowl combine and toss the oats, wheat germ, milk powder, nuts, sunflower and sesame seeds, and cinnamon.
3. In a heavy saucepan heat the honey and oil until hot but not boiling. Remove pan from heat; stir in vanilla.
4. Pour this mixture over the oats mixture and toss to coat thoroughly. Spread evenly in three 9 by 13-inch baking pans, or two roasting pans.
5. Bake for approximately 45 minutes, stirring every 15 minutes until mixture is golden.
6. Allow to cool thoroughly. Mix in the dried fruits

Cranberry Sparkler

Preparation Time: 5 minutes • Makes 1 drink

Ice
1 ounce cranberry juice
1 ounce orange juice
4 ounces club soda or seltzer
Lemon slice

Place ice in a tall glass until a third full. Mix juices with soda and pour over ice. Garnish with a slice of lemon.

Saté Babi

Our old friend Jean shared this wonderful recipe with us years ago. Now, with carefully trimmed, vacuum-packed pork tenderloins easily available, we have revived this old standby.

Preparation Time: 15 minutes • Marinating Time: Overnight • Grilling Time: About 20 minutes • Serves 6–8

1 teaspoon ground coriander
1 teaspoon ground cumin
½ cup light soy sauce
½ cup brown sugar
½ cup canola oil
3 pounds pork tenderloin, cut into 2-inch cubes
3 large onions, cut into 2-inch chunks

1. Mix together the coriander, cumin, soy sauce, brown sugar, and canola oil. Add pork and onions and marinate overnight in the refrigerator.
2. Heat grill. Alternate pork and onion chunks on skewers.
3. Barbecue until thoroughly cooked (about 20 minutes), rotating every 5 minutes to make sure the pork is cooked through.

Creamy Crunchy Potato Bake

Preparation Time: 30 minutes • Baking Time: 30 minutes • Serves 6

6 medium potatoes, peeled, boiled until just tender, and cubed (about 4½ cups)
2 cups nonfat cottage cheese
1 cup light sour cream or plain nonfat yogurt
1 large clove garlic, minced
2 green onions, finely chopped
2 tablespoons finely chopped chives
Salt and freshly ground white pepper, to taste
1 cup lightly buttered bread crumbs
1 cup lightly packed grated cheddar cheese
¼ teaspoon paprika

1. Preheat oven to 350°F. Lightly coat the inside of a 9 by 13-inch square casserole with vegetable cooking spray.
2. Toss the cooked potato cubes with the cottage cheese, sour cream, garlic, green onions, and chives. Add salt and pepper to taste and turn potato mixture into prepared casserole dish.
3. Sprinkle with bread crumbs and grated cheddar; dust with paprika. Bake for about 30 minutes until the top is golden.

Overnight Oven French Toast

The night-before assembly of this satisfying brunch dish decreases morning chaos.

Preparation Time: 20 minutes • Chilling Time: Overnight • Baking Time: About 30 minutes • Serves 8

2 tablespoons butter
8 slices raisin bread, sliced 1-inch thick (one 1-pound loaf)
4 eggs
4 egg whites
1½ cups milk
¼ cup sugar
½ teaspoon cinnamon
2 tablespoons maple syrup
1 teaspoon vanilla
½ teaspoon salt
Confectioners' sugar

1. Generously butter a large shallow baking pan and arrange the bread slices in a single layer.
2. Beat together the eggs, egg whites, milk, sugar, cinnamon, syrup, vanilla, and salt in large bowl. Pour mixture over the bread; turn slices to coat.
3. Cover with plastic wrap and refrigerate overnight.
4. Preheat oven to 400°F.
5. Bake 20 minutes or until tester inserted into center of bread comes out clean. Turn bread over and continue baking until golden, about 4 minutes longer.
6. Transfer cooked toast to warm plates and sprinkle with confectioners' sugar.

Apple Sausage Bake

Preparation Time: 30 minutes • Baking Time: 45 minutes • Serves 6

1 pound sausage links, cut in half (use turkey breakfast sausage if you find one you like)
6 tart apples, sliced but not peeled
Salt and pepper to taste
1 tablespoon lemon juice
3 tablespoons brown sugar

1. Preheat oven to 350°F. Coat a ½-quart casserole with vegetable cooking spray.

2. In a skillet, brown the sausage; drain off grease. Toss apples and sausage pieces together and put in casserole. Sprinkle with salt, pepper, lemon juice, and brown sugar.

3. Cover and bake for 45 minutes. Remove from oven, uncover, and allow to stand for 10 minutes before serving.

Arts Festival Weekend

Music, art, theater, and dance events abound in the Berkshire hills of western Massachusetts during the summer months. The Tanglewood Music Festival in Lenox, Williamstown Theater Festival in Williamstown, and Saratoga Performing Arts Center in nearby New York State, along with many smaller performing arts groups, turn this small geographic area into a bustling hub of arts activities. The usually sleepy streets of Lenox, Stockbridge, and Williamstown fill with out-of-town visitors during the summer months. The beautiful rural setting draws lovers of the outdoors as well as the performing arts. For years our friend Larrie has come for a summer weekend of culture during which we pack in as many performances as we possibly can. Besides filling ourselves with music, theater, and dance, we always seem to spend a considerable amount of time filling our tummies. Recently, she and her husband Rocky brought some wonderful Northwest salmon which we incorporated into the weekend menu.   *E.S.*

Friday
Night Arrival Snack

Build-Your-Own Tostadas with Chicken* and Black Bean Dip* • Kate's Fresh Salsa (see recipe on page 96)
Fresh Fruit

Saturday
Breakfast

Bagels with Assorted Cheeses • Coffee and Juice

Picnic Lunch at Summer Festival

Italian Bean Salad*
Fresh Tomato Basil Pizzas*
Fresh Fruit and Cookies

Dinner

Black Bean Dip and Chips
Grilled Pork Tenderloin*
Grilled Summer Vegetables • *Polenta*
Forgotten Dessert Meringues with Fresh Berries*

Sunday

Breakfast Bar

DeeDee's Best Waffles* • Fresh Fruit Slices
Juices • Assorted Coffees

Tanglewood Tea

Sliced Smoked Salmon with Yogurt Spread*
Capers, Sliced Onions, and Rye Crackers
Iced Tea, Fresh Lemonade, Sparkling Water, and Champagne

Supper

Pan Bagnat* (Grilled Bread)
Fresh Corn
Garden Salad

recipe included

THINGS TO DO AHEAD

THE WEEKEND BEFORE

■ Organize your picnic basket to include plates, tablecloth, napkins, utensils, food containers, and glasses
■ Make and freeze Black Bean Dip
■ Make dough for Tomato Basil Pizzas; roll out and freeze

WEDNESDAY

■ Make Kate's Fresh Salsa
■ Poach and chill chicken breasts for Tostadas

THURSDAY

■ Thaw Black Bean Dip
■ Prepare Italian Bean Salad
■ Prepare Summer Vegetables and store in zip-seal bags
■ Make Forgotten Dessert Meringues

FRIDAY MORNING

■ Put Meringues in airtight container
■ Wash, spin, and store salad greens

WEEKEND WORK PLAN

FRIDAY EVENING

■ Arrange the Build-Your-Own Tostadas area
■ Just before bed, set up coffee and juice area

SATURDAY MORNING

■ After breakfast, thaw pizza dough for 30 minutes, then assemble and bake pizzas
■ Pack up picnic
■ Go to a summer festival matinee performance

SATURDAY EVENING

■ Set out Black Bean Dip and Chips
■ Marinate and grill Pork Tenderloin
■ Make Polenta
■ Grill Summer Vegetables
■ Combine berries for Meringues
■ Eat and enjoy!
■ Just before bed, set up breakfast bar

SUNDAY MORNING

■ Prepare DeeDee's Best Waffles
■ Enjoy a leisurely breakfast
■ Prepare and pack up food for Tanglewood Tea
■ Assemble Pan Bagnat and chill overnight
■ Go and enjoy the concert!

SUNDAY EVENING

■ Grill the Pan Bagnat
■ Cook corn
■ Make garden salad
■ Eat a relaxing supper under the stars before your guests head home

Build-Your-Own Tostadas with Chicken and Black Bean Dip

A favorite quick supper, tostadas offer great variety in a light, healthy meal. Unlike a taco, where the tortilla is folded and filled, a tostada is built on a flat tortilla, stacked with good things. The quantities in this recipe are just a guide; feel free to adjust them to fit the number, tastes, and appetites of your guests.

Preparation time: 20 minutes • Serves 6 (flexible)

4–8 flour tortillas (depending on appetites)
1 cup Black Bean Dip (optional; see following recipe)
3 tomatoes, chopped
1 whole chicken breast, cooked and shredded
1–2 cups shredded jalapeño jack cheese, cheddar, or any other highly meltable cheese (low-fat if possible)
1 can chopped green chiles
1 cup plain nonfat yogurt
1½ cups Kate's Fresh Salsa (see recipe on page 96, or use bottled salsa)
2–4 cups shredded lettuce
Chopped green pepper, chopped onions, or anything else that you would like to add (optional)

1. Heat an iron skillet or griddle. Soften each tortilla on the griddle over medium heat for 1 minute on each side.

2. Heat the bean dip in the skillet; add 1 cup of the chopped tomatoes and warm the entire mixture, stirring frequently.

3. Spread each tortilla with 2 tablespoons of the beans and some chicken; top with about ¼ cup shredded cheese. Heat in a microwave oven on high for 30 seconds, or in a 350°F oven for 5 minutes.

4. Arrange the tostadas on a platter; serve surrounded by bowls filled with the remaining tomatoes, chiles, yogurt, salsa, and other toppings. (I like to use an assortment of handmade pottery bowls.)

5. To complete the assembly set a tostada on a plate, sprinkle with shredded lettuce, then tomatoes, then chiles. Top with a dollop of yogurt and a spoonful of salsa. These are best eaten with a knife and fork and provide a delicious well-balanced, light supper. Even those who don't care for beans love them.

(continued on next page)

Black Bean Dip

Preparation Time: 20 minutes • Cooking Time: 1½ hours
Makes 2½ cups

2 cups dried black beans
1½ quarts water
1 thin slice salt pork or bacon
3 sprigs cilantro
1 bay leaf
4 cloves garlic, crushed and peeled
1 hot pepper, seeded
Salt and freshly ground black pepper, to taste
1 tomato, chopped and seeded
2 tablespoons chopped cilantro

1. Combine the first seven ingredients in a large pot and bring to a boil. Reduce heat and simmer, partially covered, for 1½ hours until beans are tender. Add more water as needed.

2. Remove salt pork and bay leaf. Mash the beans with a potato masher or process half of them in a food processor. Combine all the beans in a bowl and season with salt, pepper, and additional cilantro. The beans may be refrigerated or frozen at this point.

3. Add tomato and chopped cilantro when ready to serve. You will have a textured mixture with some whole beans and some mashed ones. Use half of the beans in the tostados. Save the rest to serve as a dip on Saturday night before dinner.

Italian Bean Salad

Preparation Time: 20 minutes • Chilling Time: Several hours • Serves 6

Two 16-ounce cans cannellini beans, drained and rinsed
1 medium red onion, thinly sliced
3 bottled artichoke hearts, drained and quartered
⅓ cup black olives, sliced
1 teaspoon dried oregano
1 cup shredded arugula (optional)
½ teaspoon cornstarch
¼ cup chicken broth
4 tablespoons red wine vinegar
2 tablespoon extra-virgin olive oil
Salt and freshly ground pepper, to taste

1. Mix together the beans, onions, artichoke hearts, olives, oregano, and arugula in a medium bowl.

2. Combine the cornstarch and chicken broth in a small saucepan; cook over low heat until the mixture thickens, then cook for a few more minutes. Cool slightly; whisk in vinegar and oil. Pour over the bean mixture and lightly toss. Chill. Pack in a nice dish and take to the picnic. Serve at room temperature.

Fresh Tomato Basil Pizzas

Make the dough for this pizza in advance; roll it out before freezing. On the morning of the picnic, thaw the dough for 30 minutes, then assemble the pizzas and bake so they are warm when you pack them in the basket.

Preparation Time: 30 minutes • Makes six 5-inch pizzas

Rich Pizza Dough

1 tablespoon yeast
¼ cup warm water
¼ teaspoon salt
1 egg, slightly beaten
1 ½ cups all-purpose flour
1 tablespoon unsalted butter
Cornmeal, for sprinkling

Topping

¼ cup goat cheese
4 of the nicest, freshest tomatoes around, peeled and thinly sliced
½ cup finely shredded fresh basil leaves
Freshly ground black pepper
Coarse salt
Freshly grated Parmesan cheese
Full-flavored, good-quality olive oil

1. Dissolve the yeast in the warm water. Add the salt and egg and mix well. Beat in the flour and butter with a wooden spoon.

2. Knead the dough on a floured board until it is smooth and elastic. Divide into 6 equal pieces; let it sit on the board, covered lightly with a dish towel, to rise until double in size, about 30 minutes.

3. Preheat oven to 500°F (unless you plan to freeze dough).

4. Pat or roll each piece of dough into a 5-inch circle. (The crust can be frozen at this point for use later, if desired.) Roll up the edges slightly to form a small crust edge and slide onto a baking sheet or pizza stone sprinkled with cornmeal.

5. Spread a thin layer of goat cheese on each pizza. Arrange the tomatoes in an overlapping pattern on top of the cheese. Sprinkle each pizza with basil, a few grindings of pepper and salt, and fresh Parmesan; finish by drizzling olive oil over each.

6. Bake for 10 minutes, until the edges are browned and slightly puffy. Cool slightly and pack carefully in the picnic basket.

Grilled Pork Tenderloin

Preparation Time: 30 minutes • Serves 6

Two ¾-pound pork tenderloins, trimmed of fat and membrane
¼ cup orange marmalade
1 sprig fresh rosemary, or ½ teaspoon dried
¼ cup white wine vinegar
1 teaspoon grated orange rind
Salt and freshly ground pepper, to taste

1. Combine the marmalade, rosemary, vinegar, and orange rind in a small saucepan; heat until the marmalade dissolves and the mixture is well blended. Pour mixture over the tenderloins and let sit for 15 minutes.

2. Prepare the grill and brush the rack lightly with oil.

3. Grill the tenderloins for 3–5 minutes on a side, until the outside is brown and the inside just barely cooked through. Remove from the grill and brush with marinade sauce a few times. (The meat will continue to cook for a few minutes after it is removed from the grill.)

4. Slice tenderloins into $1/2$-inch slices and arrange on a large platter with sprigs of rosemary.

Grilled Summer Vegetables

Preparation Time: 20 minutes • Serves 6

6 cups assorted vegetables: eggplant, zucchini, onions (cut
into thick slices lengthwise), tomatoes, peppers, and
whatever else you have on hand
4 tablespoons chopped fresh thyme leaves, or 1 tablespoon
dried
Salt and freshly ground pepper, to taste
Extra-virgin olive oil
1 whole red or green pepper (to grill for Sunday night's
pan bagnat)

1. After cooking the grilled pork tenderloin (see recipe on page 138), lay the vegetables (except the whole pepper) on the grill and cook for a few minutes on each side until they are browned and slightly tender. Sprinkle with thyme.

2. Arrange vegetables on a platter with the pork and season with salt and pepper. Drizzle with several tablespoons of olive oil.

3. Grill the whole pepper, and when browned on all sides, put it in a paper bag for a few minutes to steam. Peel off the skin and save the pepper for Sunday supper.

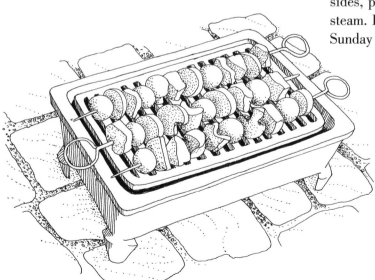

Polenta

The unknowing would refer to polenta as cornmeal mush. It is a simple Italian dish where method is everything and cooking is an act of love. Care and patience are essentials for making a good polenta. This ancient dish was a mainstay of the Roman legions who packed it up when they went on campaigns. It is adaptable to many flavors and additions. Polenta can be served soft right from the pot, cooled and fried, or baked with a variety of seasonings and additions. Here is a simple basic soft polenta.

Preparation Time: 30 minutes • Serves 6

3 cups skim milk or water
1 cup stoneground cornmeal
1 teaspoon salt
1 teaspoon butter
¼ cup freshly grated Parmesan cheese or crumbled
   gorgonzola

1. In a large heavy saucepan bring the milk or water to a simmer. Add the salt. Very slowly and in a thin stream add the cornmeal, stirring constantly with a wooden spoon. Turn down heat and cook for about 20 minutes, until the polenta thickens, stirring constantly with a wooden spoon to prevent sticking.

2. The polenta is done when it comes away from the side of the pan as you stir. Add butter and cheese and stir until they melt. Serve hot with the pork and vegetables.

Forgotten Dessert Meringues with Fresh Berries

One of my favorite ways to consume the summer's harvest of berries is in a meringue. If time and opportunity permit a few hours for picking your own in a berry patch, so much the better. In the past I topped the berries with whipped cream; now I use yogurt sauce.

Preparation Time: 30 minutes • Baking and Setting Time: 4 hours or overnight • Serves 6

4 egg whites (at room temperature)
¼ teaspoon cream of tartar
Dash of salt
¾ cup sugar
1 teaspoon vanilla

Filling

4 cups cleaned, hulled berries: strawberries, raspberries, blueberries, or whatever pleases you and is available
¼ cup sugar

Topping

½ cup plain nonfat yogurt
2 tablespoons lemon juice
2 tablespoons sugar or creme de Cassis *or*
1 cup half-and-half or heavy cream, whipped and mixed with 1 teaspoon vanilla and 2 tablespoons sugar

1. Preheat oven to 450°F.
2. Beat the egg whites, cream of tartar, and salt in a large bowl until frothy. Gradually add the sugar, a tablespoon at a time, while continuously beating. When all the sugar is added, beat until stiff glossy peaks form. Add vanilla.
3. Cover a baking sheet with parchment paper. Drop 6 large dollops of meringue on the baking sheet. With the back of a large spoon make a little nest in the center of each meringue. To be more elegant, use a large star tip on a pastry bag and pipe 8 disks, forming low walls around the outer edge of each disk.
4. Put the baking sheet in the oven and turn it off. Leave the meringues at least 4 hours or overnight without opening the door. Peel off the paper and store in an airtight container.
5. When ready to assemble, mix together the berries and sugar; let sit for a few minutes. Arrange meringues on pretty dessert plates and fill each with about a half cup of berries.
6. Mix together the yogurt, lemon juice, and sugar or Cassis. (This can be done ahead as long as you gently mix the ingredients together.) Spoon topping on each meringue and serve with great pleasure.

Tip on meringues: If egg whites are at room temperature, and you use clean beaters, the volume should increase sevenfold, giving a glorious meringue. Dry days are also better. Atmospheric moisture can make them sticky.

DeeDee's Best Waffles

This recipe exhibits another of the fine uses for plain nonfat yogurt to produce a light, delectable dish. These waffles are just plain good!

Preparation Time: 30 minutes • Makes 10 small round waffles

2 egg yolks
¾ skim milk
2 tablespoons oil
1 teaspoon vanilla
¾ cup plain nonfat yogurt
1 cup all-purpose flour
½ cup whole wheat pastry flour
½ teaspoon salt
2 teaspoons baking powder
½ teaspoon baking soda
3 egg whites

Variations: Chopped pecans, Chopped apple, Wild blueberries

1. Beat the egg yolks in a large bowl.
2. Add the milk, oil, vanilla, and yogurt; mix until frothy.
3. Sift together the flours, salt, baking powder, and baking soda and add to the milk mixture. Beat until well blended.
4. With an electric mixer and clean beaters, beat the egg whites until stiff peaks form. Stir about a quarter of the egg whites into the batter. Gently fold in the remaining egg whites.
5. Cook on a preheated waffle iron according to directions. Top with warm maple syrup. For variety, have small bowls of chopped pecans, wild blueberries, and chopped apple which people may add to their waffles before cooking. After spreading batter on the waffle iron, sprinkle a tablespoon of fruit or nuts directly on the batter and cover lightly with additional batter before cooking.

Tip on beating egg whites: A sure way to test whether egg whites are sufficiently beaten to form stiff peaks is to turn the bowl upside down — with stiff peaks the egg whites won't slide out. It is best to do this test *gradually.*

Yogurt Spread (to serve with sliced smoked salmon)

Preparation Time: 10 minutes Setting Time: Overnight • Makes 1 cup

¾ cup yogurt cheese (1½ cups plain nonfat yogurt, strained
  through cheesecloth overnight to remove liquid)
¼ cup light mayonnaise
1 tablespoon minced fresh dill
1 tablespoon lemon juice

Mix all ingredients together in a small bowl and chill.
Serve with smoked salmon on crackers.

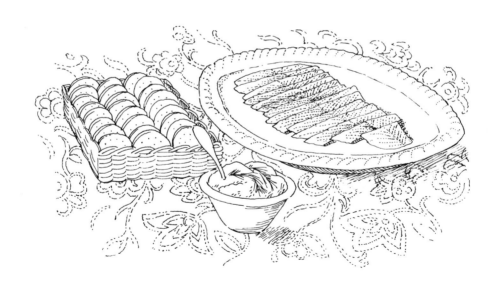

Pan Bagnat (Grilled Bread)

Preparation Time: 30 minutes • Setting Time: 30 minutes to overnight • Grilling Time: 15 minutes • Serves 4

1 loaf French bread
Olive oil
1 clove garlic, crushed

Dressing
¼ cup chopped fresh parsley
¼ cup chopped fresh basil
1 clove garlic, minced
4 anchovy fillets
2 tablespoons capers
2 tablespoons lemon juice
¼ cup olive oil

Filling
1 medium onion, thinly sliced
½ cup sliced marinated artichoke hearts
2 medium tomatoes, sliced
1 green or red pepper, roasted, peeled, and cut into chunks
12 black olives, sliced
¼ pound thinly sliced provolone cheese
1–2 thinly sliced, roasted or poached half chicken breasts

1. Cut the loaf of bread in half lengthwise; drizzle with olive oil and rub with crushed garlic.

2. With the metal blade in place, add the parsley, basil, garlic, anchovy, capers, and lemon juice to bowl of a food processor and process until evenly combined. Continue processing and gradually add the olive oil.

3. Spread the dressing on each half of the bread and layer with slices of onion, artichoke hearts, tomato, pepper, olives, cheese, and chicken.

4. Put the two bread halves together and wrap tightly in aluminum foil. Set on a cutting board and put a heavy weight on top. Chill in the refrigerator for at least 30 minutes or overnight.

5. Before serving, unwrap the sandwich and cut it in half. Place in a basket grill and toast until the bread browns and the cheese melts, about 5–10 minutes on a side. If you don't have a basket grill, very carefully place the pieces on the grill and turn with two large spatulas. Cut each piece in half and serve.

River Rafting Weekend

A few years ago, a group of our hometown friends gathered for a weekend in the Berkshire hills of Massachusetts, complete with old spouses, no spouses, and new spouses. What better way to get acquainted with the new members of the old gang than to share terror while careening through white water?

A light, quick supper for those arriving Friday night sets the weekend in motion. Marinating and grilling a hunk of meat is not only delicious, but an easy way to feed a crowd, especially after being out all day. At mealtime there are many hands to help shuck the corn and prepare vegetables as you swap stories about the river, the past, and the present. *E.S.*

Friday
Arrival Supper

Pasta and Tomato Sauce with a Twist*
Crusty Bread • Garden Salad

Saturday
Quick Breakfast
(so you can get on the river)

Assorted Cold Cereals
Fresh Fruit

Lunch

"Outfitters Delight"
(lunch on the river, supplied by the rafting company)

Dinner Buffet

Mustard Grilled Lamb* • Broiled Potatoes*
Fresh Corn • Black Beans with Fresh Tomatoes*
Julienne of Summer Vegetables* • Mixed Berry Cobbler*

Sunday
Relaxing Brunch on the Deck
with the Sunday Paper

Apple Cinnamon Stuffed French Toast*
Leftover Cobbler • Icy Orange Juice • Pots of Coffee

Lazy Late-Afternoon Lunch

Brie and Pear Pizza* • Green Garden Salad
Wine Spritzers

*recipe included

THINGS TO DO AHEAD

THE WEEKEND BEFORE

- Cook and freeze Black Beans
- Wash, spin, and store salad greens

THURSDAY

- Marinate Mustard Grilled Lamb
- Cook Broiled Potatoes and store in refrigerator
- Prepare Summer Vegetables and store in zip-seal bags

FRIDAY

- Bake Mixed Berry Cobbler

WEEKEND WORK PLAN

FRIDAY EVENING

- Prepare Pasta and Tomato Sauce with a Twist
- Warm bread
- Make garden salad
- Just before bed, set up breakfast

SATURDAY MORNING

- Complete breakfast set-up
- Enjoy the river trip!

SATURDAY EVENING

- Steam Summer Vegetables and combine with sauce
- Grill Lamb
- Complete Broiled Potatoes
- Prepare Black Beans with Fresh Tomatoes
- Boil corn
- Just before bed, set up coffee and juice area

SUNDAY MORNING

- Prepare Stuffed French Toast

SUNDAY MIDDAY

- Prepare Brie and Pear Pizzas and bake
- Make garden salad

Pasta and Tomato Sauce with a Twist

Preparation Time: 20 minutes • Serves 4

8 ounces bow-tie pasta
2 teaspoons olive oil
½ cup sun-dried tomatoes packed in oil, sliced
1 pound canned tomatoes, chopped, with their juice
Freshly ground black pepper, to taste (optional)
2 tablespoons minced fresh parsley
Freshly grated Parmesan cheese, to taste

1. Cook pasta in a large kettle of rapidly boiling salted water until al dente; drain well.
2. Meanwhile, coat the bottom of a large saucepan with the olive oil and cook sun-dried tomatoes and canned tomatoes over medium heat until the liquid evaporates slightly.
3. Add the cooked pasta and stir; cook for a few minutes to let the pasta absorb some of the flavor. Season with pepper if you wish, but taste carefully.
4. Serve in a large bowl sprinkled with parsley and cheese.

Mustard Grilled Lamb

Be sure to get a good piece of lamb and you will have a marvelous meal.

Preparation Time: 45 minutes • Marinating Time: 2–3 days • Serves 8–10

1 tablespoon dry mustard
1 tablespoon Dijon mustard
1 teaspoon sugar
3 tablespoons water
2 large cloves garlic, mashed
½ cup olive oil
2 dried red chili peppers, broken in half, sautéed briefly in
 1 tablespoon olive oil
½ cup fresh rosemary leaves, loosely packed and then
 finely chopped, or 2 tablespoons dried
¼ cup lemon juice
1 teaspoon freshly ground black pepper
½ teaspoon salt
2 teaspoons dried oregano
¼ cup red wine vinegar
Salt and pepper to taste
1 whole leg of lamb, boned and butterflied

1. Mix all the ingredients except the lamb together to make marinade and let sit for about 15 minutes.
2. Remove excess fat from lamb. Pierce the meat all over with a fork. Pour the marinade into a large shallow roasting pan. Add the lamb, cover with plastic wrap, and massage the marinade into the meat. Refrigerate the lamb for 2 or 3 days, turning occasionally.
3. One hour before grilling remove lamb from marinade and pat partially dry.
4. Preheat grill and brush lightly with oil.
5. Grill lamb for 10 to 15 minutes on a side until done to your liking (it should be slightly pink on the inside). Brush with marinade a few times, and have a spray bottle of water handy in case the olive oil ignites.
6. Slice lamb and arrange on a platter; sprinkle with salt and pepper and serve.

Grilling tip: Clean your grill after each use with a stiff wire brush.

Broiled Potatoes

Preparation Time: 30 minutes • Serves 8

10 medium-size red potatoes
½–¾ cup grated Gruyère cheese
Salt and freshly ground pepper

1. Boil potatoes in salted water until fork tender, 15–20 minutes. Allow to cool until you can handle them.
2. Preheat broiler.
3. Slice potatoes and arrange in a shallow 10-inch pie pan. Scatter cheese, salt, and pepper over the top and place pan 6 inches from the broiler unit for 5 minutes, or until cheese melts. Serve hot.

Black Beans with Fresh Tomatoes

Preparation Time: 15 minutes • Cooking Time: 2 hours • Serves 8

1 cup dried black beans
3 cups chicken stock
1 clove garlic, crushed
½ teaspoon cumin
3 sprigs cilantro
2 tablespoons good-quality olive oil
½ cup minced fresh parsley
Salt and freshly ground black pepper, to taste
8 red lettuce leaves (or other large-leaf lettuce)
3 large ripe tomatoes, sliced
Balsamic vinegar
Olive oil
A handful of basil leaves, shredded

1. In a large saucepan bring beans to a boil with chicken stock, garlic, cumin, and cilantro. Turn down and simmer, partially covered, for 1½ to 2 hours, or until the beans are tender. Add water if necessary.
2. Rinse and drain beans and toss with olive oil and parsley. Season with salt and pepper.
3. Place the lettuce leaves attractively on a platter. Arrange the tomatoes on top, drizzle with vinegar and olive oil, and sprinkle with basil. Scatter the beans over all.

Julienne of Summer Vegetables

Preparation Time: 30 minutes • Serves 8

4 cups assorted vegetables, cut into 2½ by ⅛-inch julienne
    sticks: carrots, zucchini, parsnips, kohlrabi, green onions,
    and any other vegetable that suits your taste
1 clove garlic, minced
1 tablespoon soy sauce
¼ cup chicken broth
2 tablespoons dry white wine
1 tablespoon rice vinegar
1 teaspoon cornstarch

1. Steam the julienne vegetables, adding the garlic and most delicate ones to the pot last because they cook quickest. Set aside in a large bowl.

2. Mix the soy sauce, broth, wine, vinegar, and cornstarch in a small saucepan. Cook over low heat until sauce boils. Pour over the vegetables and let sit at least 1 hour. Serve at room temperature.

Mixed Berry Cobbler

Preparation Time: 30 minutes • Baking Time: 45 minutes • Serves 8

Filling
5 cups mixed berries, including blueberries, raspberries, and blackberries
¾ cup brown sugar
⅓ cup lemon juice
½ teaspoon almond extract
2 tablespoons cornstarch
½ teaspoon cinnamon
¼ teaspoon nutmeg
½ teaspoon grated gingerroot

Biscuit Topping
1½ cups all-purpose flour
¼ cup ground almonds
¼ cup brown sugar
½ teaspoon salt
1 tablespoon baking powder
½ teaspoon baking soda
¼ cup butter
½ teaspoon vanilla
¼ cup plain nonfat yogurt
¼ cup skim milk
Vanilla frozen yogurt

1. Mix the berries and sugar together in a large saucepan. Combine the lemon juice, almond extract, and cornstarch. Add cornstarch mixture and all the spices to the berries and cook over medium heat, stirring frequently, for 5 minutes, or until mixture thickens slightly.

2. Pour berry mixture into a shallow 2-quart baking dish lightly coated with vegetable cooking spray.

3. Preheat oven to 400°F.

4. To make the topping, in a large bowl combine the flour, almonds, sugar, salt, baking powder, and baking soda. With a pastry cutter cut in the butter until mixture resembles coarse crumbs.

5. Mix the vanilla, yogurt, and milk together and quickly add to the flour mixture. Stir lightly until dry ingredients are just moistened. The dough will be sticky.

6. Cover the berries with dollops of biscuit dough, leaving spaces between them for the berries to bubble up. Bake for 40–45 minutes until the biscuit is golden and the berries bubbly. Be sure the biscuit dough is cooked through. Serve warm with vanilla frozen yogurt.

Apple Cinnamon Stuffed French Toast

Preparation Time: 30 minutes • Serves 6

4–6 large fresh apples, peeled and sliced
1 teaspoon plus 1 tablespoon butter
2 tablespoons sugar
1 teaspoon cinnamon
2 eggs, slightly beaten
1 egg white
½ cup skim milk
¼ teaspoon salt
12 slices whole wheat or oatmeal bread
Maple syrup and applesauce

1. In a large skillet sauté the apples in the teaspoon of butter until they are slightly soft, about 10 minutes. Mix the sugar and cinnamon in a small bowl and add to the apples. Cook 1 minute or until sugar melts.

2. In a deep-dish pie plate whisk the eggs, egg white, milk, and salt together until smooth.

3. Dip the slices of bread into the egg mixture; lay six of them out on a cutting board. Spread the apple mixture over the bread and cover with remaining slices to make "sandwiches." Press down slightly.

4. Melt half the tablespoon of butter in a large skillet or griddle. When butter is hot but not brown, add three of the sandwiches and cook until the bottoms are lightly browned. Turn them and lightly cook the other sides.

5. Cook remaining French toast sandwiches with remaining butter and serve hot with maple syrup and applesauce.

Brie and Pear Pizza

The Store at Five Corners in Williamstown, Massachusetts, serves up a wonderful selection of soups, salads, and sweets. This unusual pizza they make is one of my favorites for lunch, a light supper, or as an appetizer.

Preparation Time: 15 minutes • Baking Time: 15 minutes • Serves 1, or 4 as an appetizer

One 6-inch pizza round (pre-baked, such as Boboli)
2 teaspoons butter, melted and browned
Salt and white pepper, to taste
One 1 by 2-inch square brie cheese, cut into ¼-inch-thick
slices
1 ripe Anjou pear, cored and sliced
2 tablespoons toasted walnut pieces
Fresh thyme leaves

1. Preheat oven to 350°F.
2. Lightly brush pizza round with some of the browned butter. Sprinkle with salt and pepper to taste.
3. Place brie and pear slices decoratively on pizza round. Brush pear slices with remainder of browned butter.
4. Tuck a few walnut pieces in between the cheese and pears. Lightly sprinkle thyme leaves over all. Place pizza round on a sheet pan and bake for 10–15 minutes, until cheese just begins to melt. Serve hot.

Family Weekend at the Beach

August draws our family to the beach. Grandparents and grandchildren, nieces and nephews, enjoy a frenzy of fishing, wave riding, kite flying, shell collecting, and picture taking. It is wise to forget the mounds of wet towels, sandy footprints, and beach bug complaints and concentrate on the pure joy of sunshine, salt water, and time well shared.

If weather permits, cooking and eating outdoors works nicely. Food is definitely a focus on beach expeditions. The conversation about world affairs and the World Series, new books, and old friends is frequently punctuated by the age-old questions, "What's for lunch?" and "What's for dinner?" We have some answers that will please both old and young salts. *P.W.*

Friday
Dinner
Grilled Turkey Sausages
Vegetable Seafood Kebabs*
Basmati Rice (see recipe on page 2)
Sliced Garden Tomatoes
Herbed Caper Vinaigrette*
Lemonade Pie* *or* Sarah's Peanut Butter Pie*

Saturday
Breakfast
Sliced Cantaloupe, Bananas, and Small Boxes of Raisins
Whole Wheat English Muffins • All-Fruit Preserves
Break Shakes*

Lunch on the Beach
Avocado Sandwiches with Monterey Jack cheese slices,
alfalfa sprouts, sun-dried tomatoes,
fresh spinach, and olive oil on six-grain bread
Sliced Turkey Breast and Cranberry Salsa* Rolled
Up in Tortillas
Nana's Iced Tea* • Individual Juices

Dinner
Greek Garden Spread* • Crackers and Toasted Pita Triangles
Chip's Fajitas*
Make-Your-Own Yogurt Sundaes
(or maybe a trip to town for ice cream)

Sunday
Breakfast
Orange Whole Wheat Pancakes*
Applesauce • Sliced Nectarines
Hazelnut Coffee

recipe included

THINGS TO DO AHEAD

THE WEEKEND BEFORE

■ Get out beach picnic equipment

WEDNESDAY

■ Make Greek Garden Spread

THURSDAY

■ Make Lemonade Pie or Sarah's Peanut Butter Pie
■ Prepare Herbed Caper Vinaigrette
■ Prepare marinade for Vegetable Seafood Kebabs
■ Make Cranberry Salsa
■ Make Nana's Iced Tea

WEEKEND WORK PLAN

FRIDAY AFTERNOON

■ Recruit kitchen help, including: marinade maker; chopper; sandwich makers; and grill master or mistress
■ Combine seafood and marinade for Kebabs
■ Prepare vegetables for Kebabs

FRIDAY EVENING

■ Assemble Vegetable Seafood Kebabs
■ Cook Basmati Rice
■ Prepare sliced tomatoes
■ Grill Kebabs & Turkey Sausages
■ Just before bed, set up coffee and juice area

SATURDAY MORNING

■ Make Break Shakes
■ Prepare and pack sandwiches for beach

SATURDAY AFTERNOON

■ Prepare vegetables for Fajitas
■ Make marinade for Chip's Fajitas and add separately to chicken and vegetables
■ Prepare Fajitas accompaniments
■ Grill Fajitas
■ Just before bed, set up coffee and juice area

SUNDAY MORNING

■ Prepare Orange Whole Wheat Pancake batter
■ Slice nectarines and put out other breakfast foods
■ Cook Pancakes

Vegetable Seafood Kebabs

Prepare the marinade a day in advance and recruit sun-shy guests to assemble kebabs.

Preparation Time: 40 minutes • Marinating Time: 2 hours • Grilling Time: About 15 minutes • Serves 8

¾ cup olive oil
¾ cup fresh lemon juice
2 tablespoons finely chopped fresh parsley
1 tablespoon finely chopped fresh thyme
2 tablespoons grated lemon peel
1 tablespoon freshly ground black pepper
24 sea scallops
12 thin slices prosciutto, halved lengthwise
24 large shrimp, peeled
8 small white onions, peeled
3 small zucchini, cut into ¾-inch slices
16 large mushrooms
3 peppers (1 red, 1 green, and 1 yellow), cut into 1-inch squares
Cooked Basmati Rice (see recipe on page 62)

1. Whisk together olive oil, lemon juice, parsley, thyme, lemon peel, and ground pepper in a small bowl. Wrap each scallop in a prosciutto slice and secure with toothpicks. Place scallops and shrimp in a shallow dish; cover with marinade and refrigerate for at least 2 hours.

2. Cook onions in boiling water for 5 minutes. Drain.

3. Remove toothpicks from scallops and alternate seafood with vegetables on skewers.

4. Heat grill.

5. Place prepared skewers on hot grill and cook for about 8 minutes. Baste with marinade and turn once. Continue cooking for about 7 more minutes, until seafood is opaque.

6. Serve on a bed of basmati rice.

Herbed Caper Vinaigrette

Preparation Time: 10 minutes • Makes 1 cup

⅓ cup white wine vinegar
1 tablespoon lemon juice
1 teaspoon Dijon mustard
Salt and freshly ground pepper, to taste
⅔ cup extra-virgin olive oil
2 tablespoons chopped parsley
1 tablespoon chopped green onion
1 teaspoon capers
1 clove garlic, minced

1. Whisk together vinegar, lemon juice, and mustard. Season to taste with salt and pepper. Gradually blend in olive oil. Whisk in chopped parsley, green onions, capers, and garlic. **Or:** Put all the ingredients except the capers in a food processor or blender and blend at high speed. Mix in capers. Dressing can be stored in the refrigerator for several days.

Lemonade Pie

Jamie frequently requests this wonderful pie. It is a perfect recipe for beginning cooks! It is simple and satisfying, and the rave reviews that follow it may lead to more challenging culinary adventures.

Preparation Time: 15 minutes • Freezing Time: 2 hours • Makes two 9-inch pies

Two 9-inch pie shells, baked
One 10-ounce jar apricot preserves
One 6-ounce can frozen lemonade concentrate, thawed
½ gallon vanilla frozen yogurt, slightly thawed

Optional: Chocolate curls for garnish

1. Heat apricot preserves just until they become liquid. Cool slightly.

2. With a large sturdy spoon quickly blend the preserves, lemonade concentrate, and yogurt together, trying to keep the yogurt from thawing any more than is necessary.

3. Fill pie shells with yogurt mixture; cover tightly with plastic wrap and freeze until ready for use.

4. If you like, sprinkle pie with chocolate curls before serving.

Sarah's Peanut Butter Pie

Sarah works magic in a tiny Manhattan kitchen using recipes she brought with her from Louisiana. This is one of those recipes we love, where the creating is fast and fun, and the results memorable.

Preparation Time: 20 minutes • Freezer Time: 5 hours • Makes one 9-inch pie

One 9-inch graham cracker crust (see recipe on page 195)
1 quart vanilla frozen yogurt or light ice cream
⅓ cup creamy peanut butter
½ cup light corn syrup
⅔ cup unsalted dry roasted peanuts

1. Allow yogurt to soften.

2. Blend peanut butter and corn syrup together.

3. Alternate layers of yogurt, peanut butter, and peanuts in the pie crust, beginning with half the softened yogurt, half the peanut butter, and half the peanuts.

4. Cover tightly with plastic wrap and freeze for at least 5 hours before serving.

Break Shakes

Preparation Time: 5 minutes • Makes 2 shakes

8 ice cubes
1 banana
2 cups strawberries *or* 2 cups sliced, peeled peaches
1 cup plain nonfat yogurt
2 tablespoons honey

1. Crack the ice cubes with the back of a spoon and drop in a blender.

2. Add all the other ingredients to the blender and process until ice cubes are thoroughly crushed and liquid is thick and foamy (about 15 seconds). Pour into chilled glasses.

Cranberry Salsa

Although beach season and cranberry season are not one and the same, I try to keep several bags of cranberries in the freezer to break the summer tomato procession.

Preparation Time: 10 minutes • Makes 3 cups

2 large oranges
2 cups chopped cranberries (if frozen, thaw first)
1 tablespoon finely chopped green onions
¼ cup olive oil
1 tablespoon minced cilantro
1 tablespoon minced fresh gingerroot
1 small jalapeño chili pepper, seeded and minced

1. Grate 4 teaspoons orange rind from the oranges; place in a small bowl. Remove remaining peel and white membranes, coarsely chop the oranges, and let drain in a colander.

2. Toss cranberries with orange rind. Add chopped oranges, green onions, oil, cilantro, ginger, and jalapeño. Toss to blend.

3. Serve, or cover and refrigerate.

Nana's Iced Tea

This iced tea is a delicious version of one my grandmother served during screen-porch summers long ago.

Preparation Time: 1 hour, but does not need constant attention • Chilling Time: Several hours or overnight • Makes 1 gallon

3 lemons
2 oranges
12 tea bags
1 cup chopped fresh mint leaves
1 cup sugar
3½ quarts water
Mint sprigs, for garnish

1. Squeeze oranges and lemons; reserve lemon hulls. Refrigerate juices.
2. Boil 2 quarts water; remove from heat and add tea bags, mint leaves, and lemon hulls. Steep for 30 minutes. Strain mixture and blend in sugar. Refrigerate until thoroughly chilled.
3. When ready to serve, add fruit juices and 1½ quart cold water.
4. Pour into ice-filled glasses and garnish with mint sprigs.

Greek Garden Spread

This wonderful spread captures the taste of summer. If you have any leftovers, it makes a terrific sandwich spread on rye bread and topped with tomatoes.

Preparation Time: 15 minutes • Chilling Time: At least 1 hour • Serves 12

8 ounces feta cheese
One 8-ounce package low-fat cream cheese
6 ounces nonfat cottage cheese
2 tablespoons plain nonfat yogurt
1 tablespoon chopped fresh mint leaves, tightly packed, or
 ½ teaspoon dried
1 clove garlic, minced
1 medium tomato, seeded and diced
1 small cucumber, diced
1 green onion, diced
Mint leaves, for garnish
Pita triangles and crisp round crackers

1. Quickly rinse feta in cold water; pat dry and crumble. In a small mixing bowl blend the cheeses, yogurt, mint, and garlic.

2. Mound mixture in the center of a round serving plate; cover and chill thoroughly.

3. Just before serving, sprinkle spread with diced tomato, cucumber, and green onion; garnish with mint sprigs. Serve with toasted pita triangles and crisp round crackers.

Chip's Fajitas

Chip's specialty is so delicious that we don't mind if he never moves on to anything else.

Preparation Time: 30 minutes • Marinating Time: 4 hours • Grilling Time: 20–25 minutes • Serves 6

Juice of 6 limes
¾ cup olive oil
½ cup red wine vinegar
½ cup chopped cilantro
3 cloves garlic, minced
½ teaspoon crushed red pepper flakes
Two 4-ounce cans chopped chili peppers
2 pounds boneless, skinless chicken breasts
1 Spanish onion, sliced
2 red bell peppers, thinly sliced lengthwise
1 green bell pepper, thinly sliced lengthwise
1 yellow bell pepper, thinly sliced lengthwise
6 large flour tortillas

Accompaniments:
½ cup guacamole
1 cup shredded low-fat Monterey Jack cheese
½ cup low-fat sour cream mixed with ½ cup low-fat yogurt

1. In a medium mixing bowl combine the lime juice, olive oil, and vinegar. Whisk in cilantro, garlic, red pepper flakes, and green chili peppers.

2. Place the chicken in a large bowl. Top with several onion slices and scatter some pepper slices evenly over the onions. Carefully pour about 2 cups of the marinade over all. Cover with plastic wrap and refrigerate for 2 hours.

3. Put the rest of the onions and peppers in a small bowl, cover with the remaining marinade and refrigerate.

4. After 2 hours, toss the chicken and return to the refrigerator to marinate for another 2 hours.

5. Preheat the grill. Remove chicken from marinade and discard marinade.

6. Distribute chicken on grill. Pour onion/pepper marinade into a foil pan; set next to chicken on grill.

7. Grill chicken, turning two or three times and basting with marinade until thoroughly done (20–25 minutes).

8. Preheat oven to 325°F. Wrap tortillas in foil and warm in oven for about 6 minutes.

9. Remove chicken from grill and slice. Arrange on a warm platter.

10. With a slotted spoon, remove peppers and onions from the hot marinade and arrange in a bowl. Place warm tortillas in a napkin-lined basket.

11. Set out chicken, peppers and onions, tortillas, and accompaniments. Invite guests to assemble their own fajitas by putting chicken, onions and peppers, and the accompaniments of their choice on a tortilla, folding it like a taco, and enjoying their creation.

Orange Whole Wheat Pancakes

Sarah's Aunt Eugenia shared this wonderful recipe with us. The pancakes are delicious topped with a dollop of applesauce.

Preparation Time: 15 minutes for batter • Cooking Time: About 6 minutes • Makes 10 large pancakes

1 cup whole wheat flour
1 cup orange juice
1 teaspoon salt
1 teaspoon baking soda
½ cup vegetable oil
2 eggs plus 2 egg whites, whisked together
Blueberries (optional)

1. In a medium-size bowl blend together flour, juice, salt, and baking soda. Slowly add vegetable oil, mixing thoroughly. Blend in egg mixture.

2. Coat a skillet with vegetable cooking spray and heat to medium high. Pour on enough batter for desired pancake size; sprinkle with blueberries. Lower heat to medium and cook for about 2 to 3 minutes; turn pancakes over and continue cooking for another 2 to 3 minutes until golden brown.

FALL WEEKENDS

I f it is true that the best part of each season is its beginning, then fall is the prime example. At its onset, before the time of growing ends, there is a glorious display of nature's brilliance. In New England, the first hints of autumn color begin to appear in August along country roads with trees that are old and dying. It's most striking early on, when few leaves have dropped to the ground and the colored ones are set against a backdrop of green. Gradually, the vibrant color spreads across the landscape. But fall is just a moment in the year, and then it is gone.

The gardens stop producing and all those wonderful, heavy skinned vegetables are stored away for the long winter to come. It is again time to start thinking of stews and soups, but not before a few final picnics, hikes, and long walks in the crisp, clear air that is autumn's trademark. As days grow shorter and cooler, it is time to move inside and create those cozy tummy-warming meals.

Fall Foliage Hike Weekend

Fall is one of the best times to visit New England. A hike on a sunny, crisp day is a great activity for all ages. Our minimum effort/maximum reward hike features a half-mile uphill walk through the woods to an overlook on the Appalachian Trail which takes in the entire valley below and the distant mountain ranges of Vermont and New York State. In the fall, it's spectacular! These meals are designed to give you plenty of time for a weekend outdoors in the fresh air. *E.S.*

~~~~~~~~~~~~~~~~~~~~~~

Friday
Late Arrival Supper (arranged as a buffet that people can graze on as they arrive)
Herb Roasted Turkey Breast*
Baked Parsnips*
Crunchy Waldorf Salad*
Multigrain Baguette
Plum Crisp*

Saturday
Breakfast
Reprise of Plum Crisp
Eggs of Your Choice
Juice
Coffee and Tea

Packed Lunch
Turkey Sandwiches (leftover roast turkey breast on whole wheat bread, with sprouts, avocados, and honey mustard)
Fresh Oranges (cut in quarters)
• Cranberry Gorp* • Water

Dinner
Make-Your-Own Veggie Pizza* with Assorted Toppings
Garden Salad • Fruit Sundaes*

Sunday
Breakfast
Power Pancakes*
Cantaloupe Slices
Juices • Coffee

recipe included

THINGS TO DO AHEAD

THE WEEKEND BEFORE

- Get out backpacks and containers for a picnic in a pack
- Make Cranberry Gorp (and hide it from yourself!)
- Make and freeze dough for Veggie Pizza

WEDNESDAY

- Thaw Turkey Breast (if you purchased a frozen one)
- Grate cheese for Pizza and freeze

THURSDAY

- Make Plum Crisp
- Cut and chop Pizza toppings

FRIDAY

- Wash, spin, and store salad greens
- Organize toppings for Fruit Sundaes

WEEKEND WORK PLAN

FRIDAY EVENING

- Roast Turkey Breast and slice
- Bake Parsnips
- Prepare Waldorf Salad
- Warm bread when guests arrive
- Just before bed, set up coffee and juice area

SATURDAY MORNING

- Cook eggs, or let guests cook their own
- Make sandwiches, with help from guests
- Pack lunches
- Thaw dough and cheese for Pizza

SATURDAY EVENING

- Arrange toppings for Pizzas
- Roll out Pizza dough
- Make garden salad
- Let everyone fix their own Pizza
- Bake Pizzas
- Set out toppings for Fruit Sundaes
- Just before bed, set up coffee and juice area

SUNDAY MORNING

- Prepare Pancakes
- Complete breakfast area set-up
- Cook Pancakes; keep in warm oven for late sleepers

Herb Roasted Turkey Breast

A fairly simple way to provide a light supper is to roast a turkey breast, which can also be used for sandwiches the next day. Serve it buffet style sliced thinly. If preferred, roast it a day ahead and serve it cold. Save the bones and make turkey stock to use in soups. It's a great meal for guests.

Preparation Time: 15 minutes • Baking Time: 2½ hours • Serves 12

5–5½ pound turkey breast (Buy a whole breast, not a boneless one, if you're inclined to make turkey stock.)
2 tablespoons unsalted butter
1 tablespoon dried tarragon
1 tablespoon dried oregano
½ teaspoon salt
Freshly ground pepper
1 medium onion
Additional dried tarragon and oregano, for sprinkling

1. Preheat oven to 325°F.
2. Rinse the turkey with cold water and pat dry.
3. Combine the butter, tarragon, oregano, salt, and pepper in a small bowl to form a paste. Spread the paste over the outside of the turkey.
4. Lay the onion in the cavity with a few sprinkles of the herbs; center the breast on a rack in a shallow roasting pan. Roast for about 2½ hours, or until a meat thermometer registers 185°F. Baste occasionally.
5. Set the turkey on a large serving platter. After it has set for 10 minutes, slice one side and arrange slices on the platter.

Baked Parsnips

These can be baked along with the turkey breast.

Preparation Time: 20 minutes • Baking Time: 30 minutes • Serves 8

1 pound (about 8) parsnips, peeled, cut in half, and sliced lengthwise in equal-size pieces
½ cup skim milk
½ cup grated low-fat cheddar cheese
½ cup chopped fresh parsley
1 teaspoon butter

1. Steam the parsnips until tender crisp, 5–8 minutes. Arrange in a shallow casserole coated with vegetable cooking spray.
2. Mix the milk, cheese, and parsley together; pour over parsnips and dot with butter. Cover casserole with foil and bake with the turkey breast for the last 30 minutes or until tender, or bake separately at 325°F for 30 minutes. Serve warm with the turkey.

Crunchy Waldorf Salad

Preparation Time: 15 minutes • Serves 8

2 tart red apples
2 Granny Smith apples
3 stalks celery, diced
½ cup red seedless grapes, cut in half
½ cup green seedless grapes, cut in half
⅓ cup chopped walnuts, toasted

Dressing
½ cup plain nonfat yogurt
¼ cup light mayonnaise
¼ cup crumbled blue cheese
2 tablespoons lemon juice

1. In a large bowl toss the salad ingredients together.
2. In a small bowl stir the dressing ingredients together until smooth. Pour over the salad and mix well. Chill in the refrigerator and serve in a pretty bowl.

Plum Crisp

Make two pans and save one for Sunday breakfast.

Preparation Time: 20 minutes • Baking Time: 30 minutes • Serves 6

2 pounds mixed, firm plums (about 7 plums), cut into eighths
⅓ cup brown sugar
¼ teaspoon ground cloves
½ teaspoon cinnamon
1 tablespoon grated orange rind
1 teaspoon Amaretto

Topping
¼ cup flour
½ cup rolled oats, whirled in a blender for a few seconds
⅓ cup sugar
2 tablespoons butter
1 teaspoon cinnamon
French vanilla yogurt *or* vanilla frozen yogurt

1. Preheat oven to 375°F.
2. In a medium-size bowl toss the plums with sugar, cloves, cinnamon, orange rind, and Amaretto. Pour into a 9-inch glass pie pan coated with vegetable cooking spray and let sit while you mix the topping.
3. Mix the topping ingredients together with a fork until well blended. Sprinkle the topping over the plums; bake for 30 minutes, until the top is browned and the fruit tender.
4. Serve hot, warm, or at room temperature with the yogurt or frozen yogurt on the side.

Cranberry Gorp

Gorp is that wonderful combination of high-energy dried fruits, nuts, and chocolate that is the second reason for hiking.

Preparation Time: 10 minutes • Makes 2½ cups

1 cup sweetened dried cranberries
½ cup raisins
½ cup semisweet chocolate chunks (buy a hunk of chocolate and break into random-size chunks)
1½ cups unsweetened banana chips

Mix all ingredients together in a large bowl. Divide into zip-sealed plastic bags for each hiker and pack up with the sandwiches.

Make-Your-Own Veggie Pizza

Of course you can offer the usual meat toppings, but be creative and offer a variety of wonderful veggies. Make as many batches of dough as you think you will need. Extra dough keeps very well in the freezer. During the cooler months, we have pizza once a week. It's great to be able to grab a hunk of dough from the freezer, roll it, and create toppings from whatever is in the pantry or refrigerator at the time. People of all ages love pizza and can join in the fun of preparation.

Preparation Time: 30 minutes • Baking Time: 10–20 minutes • Serves 8
Makes two 12-inch pizzas; four 8-inch pizzas; or ten 4-inch pizzas

Dough
1 tablespoon active dry yeast
1 cup warm water
1 teaspoon sugar
½ teaspoon salt
2 tablespoons olive oil
2 cups all-purpose flour
½ cup whole wheat flour (this gives the dough an interesting texture and flavor, as well as adding nutritional value)
1 tablespoon cornmeal

Toppings
Plain canned tomato sauce (Contadina is an excellent choice)
Dried oregano
Dried or fresh chopped basil
Pesto
Red pepper flakes
Grated part-skim mozzarella, or a combination of Gruyère and cheddar cheeses
Freshly grated Parmesan cheese
Crumbled feta cheese

Grated cheddar cheese (adds a little "umph" to the flavor of mozzarella)
Chopped, steamed broccoli
Sliced artichokes hearts
Thinly sliced green pepper
Thinly sliced onions
Sliced fresh tomatoes (scrumptious!)
Sliced mushrooms, any variety you choose
Anything else that appeals to you

To make the dough:

1. In a large bowl dissolve the yeast in the warm water. Stir in the sugar, salt, oil, and flour. With a wooden spoon beat the dough vigorously for 20 strokes.

2. Scrape the dough onto a floured counter and knead it until smooth.

3. Let the dough rest for 5 minutes before rolling out. This is an important step because it allows the dough to relax, making it easier to roll.

(continued on next page)

4. Divide the dough in half; roll each half into a 12-inch circle on a floured surface. Lift the dough onto a baking sheet or pizza pan sprinkled with 1 tablespoon cornmeal. Have each guest decorate their own section, or divide the dough into smaller pieces so they can make truly individual pizzas.

To assemble:
1. Preheat oven to 475°F.
2. Spread your favorite toppings on the waiting pizza dough. A good order is a thin layer of sauce, herbs, cheese, and then other items.
3. Bake for 10–20 minutes, depending on the size, or until the dough is lightly browned and the cheese is melted.

Fruit Sundaes

Preparation Time: 15 minutes • Serves 8

1 quart vanilla nonfat yogurt
2 cups granola cereal, for sprinkling on top (see recipe for Glorious Granola on page 128)
A selection of any or all of the following, for a total of at least 4 cups:
2 cups pineapple chunks packed in juice, drained
2 cups frozen unsweetened strawberries, raspberries, or blueberries, slightly thawed
2 cans mandarin oranges, drained
2 cups seasonal fresh fruit, cut into ½-inch chunks
Anything else you think would be good

1. Set out dessert dishes.
2. Place the yogurt in a large serving bowl, the granola in another bowl, and arrange the fruits in smaller bowls. Let people create their own sundae starting with fruit, followed by yogurt, and topped with granola.

Power Pancakes

Light and delicious! These pancakes are a great way to start the day. The recipe can easily be doubled.

Preparation Time: 20 minutes • Cooking Time: 15 minutes • Serves 4

1 cup all-purpose flour
¼ cup whole wheat pastry flour
¼ cup wheat germ
½ teaspoon baking powder
½ teaspoon baking soda
¼ teaspoon salt
1 tablespoon sugar
1 egg
2 egg whites
1 cup buttermilk
1 tablespoon oil

1. Mix together the all-purpose flour, whole wheat flour, wheat germ, baking powder, baking soda, salt, and sugar in a small bowl.

2. In a large bowl whisk the eggs and egg whites until they are light and frothy. Pour some of the flour mixture into the eggs and stir well. Add some buttermilk and stir again. Repeat steps until all the flour and buttermilk are mixed into the eggs. Add the oil and mix again.

3. Place a large skillet or griddle over medium heat for a few minutes. Test the temperature of the skillet by splashing a few drops of water on the surface. If the water "dances," the skillet is the right temperature for cooking pancakes.

4. Spoon enough batter for one pancake onto the hot griddle. Let each pancake cook several minutes, until bubbles form on the top and the bottom is golden brown, before turning. To serve everyone at once, arrange the pancakes on an ovenproof platter as they come off the griddle and keep in a 200°F oven until the crowds are assembled.

5. Serve with maple syrup, butter, yogurt, jam, or whatever pleases you.

Note: For blueberry pancakes, omit the baking soda, increase the amount of baking powder to 1 teaspoon, substitute skim milk for buttermilk, and add 1 cup blueberries to the batter. You can also use the recipe as is, adding blueberries to each pancake as it cooks, but be forewarned that blueberries react chemically to baking soda, giving the pancakes a greenish tinge. Baking soda is necessary when using buttermilk, so either alter the recipe or prepare your guests for slightly strange-colored, although fine-tasting, pancakes.

Fall Reunion Weekend

Fall reunion weekends imply a football game at the old college, but many groups can get together to share meals for a fall weekend. John and Martha regularly fill their home with people of all ages. One special event is an annual gathering of campers — past, present, and future. Martha orders a 6-foot sub from the local supermarket and combines it with her wonderful spicy, fresh tomato soup to feed the crowd. Guests bring a variety of desserts which, all together, makes a great meal, and gives the cook time to prepare additional meals for those who are spending the night at the house. *E.S.*

~~~~~~~~~~~~~~~~~

Friday
Supper
Locro de Trigo (Jan's Argentina Stew)*
Crusty French Bread • Green Garden Salad
Apple Walnut Cobbler*

Saturday
Breakfast
Leftover Apple Walnut Cobbler
Basic Breakfast Bar Set-up (see page 3)

Tailgate Lunch
Harvest Bisque* • Multigrain Baguettes
Thinly Sliced Roast Beef and Horseradish
Apples and Oatmeal Date Bars*

After-the-Game Supper for a Crowd
6-foot-long sub
(ordered from your local supermarket or delicatessen)
Martha's Tomato Soup*
Leftover Oatmeal Date Bars
(and assorted brownies and cookies brought by guests)
Coffee and Tea

Sunday
Breakfast Bar
Bagels with Cream Cheese, Smoked Whitefish, Thinly Sliced
Red Onions, and Capers
Fresh Fruit, Yogurt, and Granola
Muffins
Juices

recipe included

THINGS TO DO AHEAD

THE WEEKEND BEFORE

- Get out picnic basket and equipment for tailgate picnic
- Make and freeze Apple and Oatmeal Date Bars
- Order 6-foot-long sub from your local supermarket or delicatessen

WEDNESDAY

- Make Locro de Trigo, except for adding the corn; refrigerate

THURSDAY

- Prepare Apple Walnut Cobbler
- Make Harvest Bisque and Martha's Tomato Soup; refrigerate
- Wash, spin, and store greens for garden salad

WEEKEND WORK PLAN

FRIDAY EVENING

- Warm Locro de Trigo and add corn
- Prepare salad
- Warm bread
- Just before bed, set up coffee and juice area, along with Basic Breakfast Bar Set-up

SATURDAY MORNING

- Complete Breakfast Bar Set-up
- Warm Harvest Bisque and pack in thermos
- Pack Tailgate Lunch picnic food
- Enjoy the game!

SATURDAY AFTERNOON

- Pick up 6-foot-long sub

SATURDAY EVENING

- Warm Martha's Tomato Soup
- Set out the sub
- Arrange the buffet area
- Set up area for desserts and coffee
- Just before bed, set up coffee and juice and breakfast bar

SUNDAY MORNING

- Complete breakfast bar set-up
- Wind down the weekend with a leisurely breakfast

Locro de Trigo (Jan's Argentina Stew)

We asked my son-in-law Jezz about his favorite foods from East Anglia, England, where he grew up. He recalled his mum's Argentina stew, for which Jan kindly provided the recipe. It's a delicious, colorful cool-weather stew. We have not found English garlic sausage readily available, but hot Italian turkey sausage is an excellent substitute. Canadian bacon is the closest to a "rasher" that Jezz has found in the United States.

Preparation Time: 30 minutes • Cooking Time: 2½ hours • Serves 6

1 tablespoon olive oil
2 onions, chopped
1 red pepper, seeded and chopped
1½ pounds lean beef round, cut into 1-inch cubes
1 quart beef stock
2 teaspoons paprika
One 16-ounce can baby lima beans or butter beans, drained, or one 10-ounce package frozen lima beans
6 slices Canadian bacon, diced
2 garlic sausages, sliced (½–¾ pound), or use hot Italian turkey sausages
½ teaspoon salt
¼ teaspoon black pepper
One 10-ounce package frozen corn

1. In a Dutch oven heat the olive oil over medium heat and sauté the onions, pepper, and beef for about 5 minutes.
2. Combine the stock, paprika, and beans and add to the pot; bring to a boil.
3. Lightly brown the bacon and sausage, remove some of the fat, and add to the pot. Reduce heat; cover and simmer for 2 hours, until the meat is tender and flavors well blended. Season with salt and pepper.
4. Add corn and cook for 30 minutes more over low heat. Serve hot.

Apple Walnut Cobbler

One of the all-time best cobblers!

Preparation Time: 30 minutes • Baking Time: 55 minutes • Serves 8

¼ cup sugar
½ teaspoon cinnamon
½ cup coarsely chopped walnuts
4 large, tart apples, peeled and thinly sliced to
    make 4–5 cups

Topping

1 cup all-purpose flour
¾ cup sugar
1 teaspoon baking powder
¼ teaspoon salt
1 egg
⅔ cup evaporated skimmed milk
3 tablespoons butter, melted

1. Preheat oven to 325°F.
2. In a small bowl mix the ¼ cup of sugar with the cinnamon and all but 1 tablespoon of the walnuts. Coat a deep-dish, 9-inch pie pan with vegetable cooking spray and spread the apples over the bottom. Sprinkle the cinnamon mixture over the apples.
3. Sift the dry ingredients together into a medium-size bowl. Combine the egg, milk, and butter in a small bowl. Add them all at once to dry ingredients and mix until smooth. Pour the batter over the apples and sprinkle with remaining walnuts.
4. Bake for 55 minutes, or until golden brown and apples are tender. Spoon the warm cobbler onto dessert plates and serve.

Harvest Bisque

Preparation Time: 45 minutes • Serves 8

1 large leek, cleaned, the white part chopped
1 medium onion, chopped
2 stalks celery, diced
2 large apples, peeled, cored, and chopped (Granny Smiths are a good variety)
7 cups chicken or turkey stock (see recipe on page 205)
1 tablespoon cornstarch
4 cups peeled, diced butternut squash
1 teaspoon dried thyme
½ teaspoon salt
1 teaspoon rubbed sage
¼ teaspoon turmeric
¼ teaspoon dried rosemary
1 teaspoon grated fresh gingerroot
Dash of nutmeg
Freshly ground black pepper, to taste
1 cup apple cider
½ cup plain nonfat yogurt
1 cup grated low-salt cheddar cheese (optional)

1. In a large kettle or stockpot gently steam the leeks, onion, celery, and apples in ½ cup of the stock until soft, about 10 minutes.

2. Mix the cornstarch into another ½ cup of the stock and stir until well mixed. Add the cornstarch mixture, squash, and remaining stock to the vegetables; cook over medium heat until soup boils and thickens slightly. Turn down heat and cook until squash is tender, 10–15 minutes.

3. Season the soup with the herbs and spices and cook another 5 minutes, stirring to blend the flavors.

4. Process about three-quarters of the soup in a food processor and return to the kettle. Stir in the cider and yogurt. Serve hot in soup bowls, each sprinkled with a little cheese.

Oatmeal Date Bars

This is a slight modification of a recipe from Linda England and John Angeline, the talented bakers at Wadsworth's Bakery in Princeton, New Jersey, who are famous for their muffins (see page 187). These bars are very rich indeed; cut them small and try to control yourself.

Preparation Time: 30 minutes • Baking Time: 30 minutes • Makes 24 small bars

Filling
8 ounces dates, chopped (about 1½ cups)
1½ cups water
1 cup granulated sugar
2 teaspoons grated lemon rind

Crust
2 cups all-purpose flour
½ teaspoon salt
2½ cups old-fashioned oats
½ cup finely chopped walnuts
1 cup brown sugar
¾ cup unsalted butter, melted
½ cup canola oil

1. In a small saucepan combine the dates, water, sugar, and lemon rind. Bring to a boil; lower heat and cook, stirring occasionally, until the mixture is thick and most of the water has been absorbed, about 15 minutes. Cool.
2. Preheat oven to 350°F.
3. Combine flour, salt, oats, walnuts, and brown sugar. Add melted butter and oil and toss until mixture is crumbly. Set aside 1½ cups of the crust mixture.
4. Press remaining crust mixture into the bottom of a greased 9 by 13-inch pan coated with vegetable cooking spray. Spread date mixture over crust. Sprinkle reserved crust mixture over the top of the date filling.
5. Bake for about 30 minutes, or until top is brown. Cool in pan on wire rack. Cut when cool.

Martha's Tomato Soup

Preparation Time: 30 minutes • Serves 6

1 large onion, chopped
2 slices bacon, diced
10 peppercorns
10 whole cloves
2 tablespoons brown sugar
6 cups fresh tomatoes, peeled and chopped (canned
    tomatoes can be substituted)
2 tablespoons butter
2 tablespoons flour
2 cups chicken or turkey stock
½ cup evaporated skimmed milk
½ cup half-and-half

1. In a Dutch oven cook the onion and bacon until onion is translucent and bacon is crisp. Remove all but about 1 tablespoon bacon fat.

2. Add peppercorns, cloves, and brown sugar and simmer for several minutes, stirring constantly. Stir in tomatoes and cook for 10 minutes.

3. Remove tomato mixture from heat and puree in batches in a blender. Remove large pieces of cloves and peppercorns. Set aside in a large bowl.

4. In the Dutch oven make a roux by melting the butter and stirring in the flour. Cook for 1 minute; add the stock. Cook until thickened, stirring frequently.

5. Add the tomato mixture and heat, but do not boil. Swirl in the milk and cream at the last minute and serve piping hot.

College Kids Come Home

When your students come home with new friends and old laundry, try to avoid typical college fare. Our menu suggestions are designed to accommodate both delicate and hearty appetites, as well as late arrivals and late sleepers. With a college crowd, Saturday breakfast easily blends into Saturday lunch, and activities like shopping trips or basketball games may make three standard mealtimes impractical. The meals in this menu can be scheduled flexibly. And, when the weekend comes to an end on Sunday, you can pack the delicious leftovers into a cooler for the kids' trip back to school, including fruit and cookies from Friday night's dinner, bagels with ham and cream cheese, and muffins. Add individual bottles of mineral water and a thermos of hot coffee or cocoa. *P.W.*

Friday
Late Arrival Meal
Antipasto* with Basil Vinaigrette*
Crusty Italian Bread
Fresh Fruit Bowl
Three-Chocolate Chunk Cookies*

Saturday
Morning/Afternoon Meal (probably late!)
Fruit Juices
Assorted Bagels with Smoked Salmon, Light Cream Cheese,
Thinly Sliced Baked Ham, and Fontina Cheese
Tomatoes and Sliced Red Onion
Earl Grey Tea, Coffee

Evening Meal
South-of-the-Border Lasagna*
Assorted Toppings*
Coffee Frozen Yogurt
Salsa de Chocolate*

Sunday
Breakfast
Assorted Juices
Creamy Scrambled Eggs*
Wadsworth's Muffins*
Coffee

recipe included

THINGS TO DO AHEAD

THE WEEKEND BEFORE
- Bake and freeze Three-Chocolate Chunk Cookies
- Bake and freeze Wadsworth's Muffins

WEDNESDAY
- Prepare Salsa de Chocolate

THURSDAY
- Prepare Basil Vinaigrette for Antipasto

FRIDAY
- Assemble South-of-the-Border Lasagna, but don't bake; refrigerate
- Prepare Lasagna Toppings
- Cut up fresh fruit
- Marinate artichoke hearts and mushrooms for Antipasto
- Thaw Three-Chocolate Chunk Cookie

WEEKEND WORK PLAN

FRIDAY EVENING
- Assemble Antipasto
- Arrange Chunk Cookies on serving plate
- Assemble fresh fruit bowl
- Arrange bread in basket
- Just before bed, set up coffee and juice area

SATURDAY MORNING
- Set out breakfast bar

SATURDAY EVENING
- Bake Lasagna
- Set jar of Salsa de Chocolate in warm water to heat gently
- Just before bed, remove Muffins from freezer and set up coffee and juice area

SUNDAY MORNING
- Warm Wadsworth's Muffins
- Set up breakfast area
- Prepare Creamy Scrambled eggs

Antipasto with Basil Vinaigrette

This is a good dish for weary students starting a relaxing weekend. They can nibble or stuff themselves as they like, and the leftovers can reappear the next day if needed. The key to success lies in the quality of all the ingredients.

Preparation Time: 30 minutes • Serves 8–10

1 cup basil vinaigrette
1 pound medium-size mushrooms, cleaned and trimmed
One 14-ounce can artichoke hearts, drained
One 16-ounce can hearts of palm, cut into 1-inch pieces
¾ pound cherry tomatoes
½ pound salami, cut into ½-inch cubes
1 pound Italian Fontina (or other hard cheese), cut into ½-inch cubes
One 16-ounce can jumbo black olives, drained
2 loaves sourdough French bread, or Italian semolina bread

1. Pour vinaigrette into a small bowl and mix in the artichoke hearts and mushrooms. Marinate overnight.

2. At least 1 hour before serving, combine the hearts of palm, cherry tomatoes, salami, cheese, and olives with the vinaigrette mixture in a large bowl and toss.

3. To serve, allow guests to ladle portions into individual bowls; accompany with chunks of fresh crusty Italian bread for dunking.

Basil Vinaigrette

Preparation Time: 10 minutes • Makes 2 cups

½ cup red wine vinegar
1 teaspoon Dijon mustard
1 clove garlic, minced
1½ cups extra-virgin olive oil
1 tablespoon chopped fresh basil, or 1 teaspoon dried
1 tablespoon chopped fresh oregano, or 1 teaspoon dried
Salt and freshly ground pepper

1. In a small bowl whisk vinegar, mustard, and garlic together.

2. Slowly add the oil, whisking constantly. Stir in the herbs; season to taste with salt and pepper. Store in a tightly sealed jar in refrigerator.

Three-Chocolate Chunk Cookies

There is no way we can call these deliciously rich cookies either light or healthy. Just try to practice restraint!

Preparation time: 30 minutes • Baking Time: 12 minutes • Makes 4 dozen

1 cup butter
1 cup granulated sugar
1 cup light brown sugar
1 egg
2 egg whites
1 teaspoon vanilla
2½ cups rolled oats
2 cups whole wheat pastry or unbleached all-purpose flour
1 teaspoon baking soda
1 teaspoon baking powder
1 cup milk chocolate chips
1 cup semisweet chocolate chips
4 ounces white chocolate, grated
1½ cups walnuts, coarsely chopped

1. Preheat oven to 375°F.
2. In a large bowl cream together butter and sugars. Add egg, egg whites, and vanilla. Using a blender or food processor, grind oats until fine.
3. Sift together flour, ground oats, baking soda, and baking powder. Slowly add oats and flour mixture to butter/sugar mixture and blend thoroughly.
4. Add chips, white chocolate, and walnuts; mix well.
5. Drop batter by the tablespoon onto an ungreased cookie sheet, 2 inches apart. Bake for 12 minutes, or until golden brown. Cool on wire racks. For softer cookies, remove from the oven after 10 minutes and allow to cool on cookie sheet.

South-of-the-Border Lasagna

Tana has taken the wonderful flavors of the Southwest with her from New Mexico to Minneapolis, where she brightens the long winters with creative, healthy cooking.

Preparation Time: 45 minutes • Baking Time: 30 minutes • Serves 8–10

2 pounds ground turkey
1 medium onion, chopped
1 clove garlic, minced
2 tablespoons chili powder
3 cups canned tomato sauce
One 4-ounce can chopped green chilies
12 corn tortillas
2 cups small curd nonfat cottage cheese
1 egg
2 cups grated light Monterey Jack cheese
½ cup grated cheddar cheese

Toppings
½ cup chopped green onions
½ cup light sour cream mixed with ½ cup low-fat yogurt
½ cup sliced black olives

1. Preheat oven to 350°F.
2. In a heavy skillet brown meat over medium heat; add onions and garlic and cook until tender. Sprinkle with chili powder, and mix well.
3. Stir in tomato sauce and green chilies; simmer over medium heat for 15 minutes.
4. While mixture simmers, dip the tortillas in it to soften them. Remove and set aside.
5. Beat together the cottage cheese and egg and set aside.
6. In a 9 by 13-inch casserole spread a layer of one-third of the meat mixture, top with a layer of one-half of the jack cheese, then one-half of the cottage cheese, and one-half of the tortillas. Repeat this process, ending with a layer of meat sauce. Top with grated cheddar.
7. Bake for 30 minutes.
8. Place toppings in individual bowls and and serve with lasagna.

Salsa de Chocolate

We have taken most of the guilt out of this delightful dark, glossy sauce without sacrificing a bit of flavor. A little goes a long way. You can make a batch ahead of time and just heat gently when ready to use.

Preparation Time: 15 minutes • Makes about 1½ cups

¾ cup evaporated skimmed milk
¼ teaspoon cinnamon
3 tablespoons unsalted butter
3 ounces sweet chocolate (Mexican, if you can find it)
¼ cup brown sugar
⅓ cup unsweetened cocoa powder

1. Gently heat the milk, cinnamon, and butter in a 2-quart saucepan.
2. Roughly chop the chocolate and add to the saucepan. As the chocolate melts, whisk the mixture thoroughly.
3. When smooth, add sugar and then cocoa powder, stirring well. Serve warm over coffee frozen yogurt.

Creamy Scrambled Eggs

Preparation Time: 20 minutes • Serves 8

10 eggs
4 egg whites
¼ cup skim milk
½ pound light cream cheese, diced
¼ cup chopped fresh basil, or 1 teaspoon dried
¼ cup chopped fresh parsley
1 teaspoon oregano
1 teaspoon unsalted butter

1. In a large bowl whisk eggs and egg whites together. Beat in milk, cream cheese, basil, parsley, and oregano.
2. Melt butter in a heavy skillet, add the egg mixture, and cook over low heat for about 5 minutes, stirring constantly. Serve immediately.

Wadsworth's Muffins

Wadsworth's Bakery is a Princeton, New Jersey, favorite, with muffins that are legendary. Their Victorian storefront is nestled on the side of the university campus. Every morning, students and faculty alike stop in to check the day's muffin choices and select their favorites. Wadsworth's bakers Linda England and John Angeline were kind enough to share their recipe with us, and we have altered it only slightly.

Preparation Time: 20 minutes • Baking Time: 20–30 minutes • Makes 8 medium muffins

1¾ cups all-purpose flour (substitute ½ cup with whole wheat pastry flour if desired)
½ cup sugar
1 tablespoon baking powder
½ teaspoon salt
Spices (see below for variations)
1 egg
¾ cup vegetable oil, or ½ cup oil and ⅓ cup applesauce
½ cup skim milk
½ cup plain nonfat yogurt
½ teaspoon vanilla
Additions (see next page for variations on recipe)

1. Preheat oven to 400°F.
2. Sift flour, sugar, baking powder, salt, and spices together into a large bowl.
3. In a medium bowl beat together the egg, vegetable oil, applesauce (if used), milk, yogurt, and vanilla. Pour these wet ingredients into the dry mixture, stirring just until the ingredients are barely combined.
4. Gently fold in any additions for the selected variation. Distribute them evenly throughout the batter with as few strokes as possible, then stop.
5. Immediately spoon the batter into greased or paper-lined muffin tins. Bake 20 to 30 minutes, or until a tester inserted into the center of the muffin comes out clean. Baking time will vary greatly depending on the variation. Rotate baking tin 180 degrees halfway through the baking process.

Raspberry Hazelnut

1 cup fresh or frozen raspberries
½ teaspoon ground cinnamon
½ cup toasted, chopped hazelnuts

Add raspberries to batter. Top muffins with cinnamon sugar and/or more chopped hazelnuts before baking.

Apple Walnut

½ teaspoon cinnamon
¼ teaspoon nutmeg
1⅓ cups peeled and diced apples
½ cup chopped walnuts (reserve 2 tablespoons for topping)

Add all ingredients except 2 tablespoons of walnuts to batter. Finely chop the reserved walnuts and sprinkle on top of muffins before baking.

Blueberry Crumb

1 cup fresh or frozen blueberries

Add blueberries to batter. Top muffins with a mixture of ½ cup flour, ½ cup sugar, a pinch of salt, and ¼ cup butter rubbed together to resemble coarse crumbs.

Lemon Poppy Seed

2 tablespoons poppy seeds
Grated rind of 1 lemon

Add both ingredients to batter.

Banana Bran

½ cup unprocessed bran
1 cup mashed banana

Add bran to dry ingredients (step 2). Add banana to wet ingredients (step 3).

Family in the City

Next to the beach, the city is one of the best places to take kids, as long as you plan your activities and meals well. Start with a good breakfast and find an inexpensive, fun restaurant for a lunchtime bowl of soup and hearty roll. A high tea in the late afternoon is a great way for kids and adults to unwind. This weekend is designed for those lucky folks who live in the city, like to cook, and want to invite friends for a weekend in the big city. *E.S.*

Saturday
Breakfast
Shredded Wheat and Bananas
Orange Juice
Toast and Strawberry Jam

High Tea
Assorted Finger Sandwiches*
Meg's Scones (see recipe on page 64)
English Tea

Dinner
Lemon Soup*
Braised Lamb with Vegetables*
Baked French Fries* or Crusty Bread
Spinach Cucumber Salad with Lime Dressing*
Frozen Lemon Chiffon Pie*

Sunday
Breakfast
Basic Breakfast Bar Set-up (see page 3)
Wadworth's Muffins (see recipe on page 187) with
Marscapone Cheese • Eggs Cooked to Order
Juices

recipe included

THINGS TO DO AHEAD

THE WEEKEND BEFORE

- Make and freeze Wadsworth's Muffins
- Make and freeze Meg's Scones

THURSDAY

- Prepare Braised Lamb with Vegetables; refrigerate
- Prepare Lemon Soup, except for addition of eggs, and refrigerate
- Wash, spin, and store greens for Spinach Cucumber Salad

FRIDAY

- Make and freeze Lemon Chiffon Pie
- Make and chill Finger Sandwiches

SPECIALTY ITEMS NEEDED

- Marscapone cheese

WEEKEND WORK PLAN

SATURDAY MORNING

- Set up the breakfast area
- Thaw Scones and Muffins
- Have fun in the city — go to the zoo, the aquarium, the park, or a performance

LATE SATURDAY

- Set out Finger Sandwiches and Scones
- Make tea, serve with milk and sugar

FOR LATE SATURDAY DINNER

- Get kids to help cut potatoes
- Bake French Fries
- Complete Lemon Soup
- Warm Braised Lamb
- Prepare Spinach Cucumber Salad
- Warm bread
- Remove Lemon Chiffon Pie from freezer and, while eating dinner, allow it to thaw
- Just before bed, set up Breakfast Bar

SUNDAY MORNING

- Complete Breakfast Bar Set-up
- Cook eggs to order

Finger Sandwiches

Preparation Time: 30 minutes • Serves 8

1 loaf unsliced white bread (from bakery)
1 loaf unsliced whole wheat bread (from bakery)
2 tablespoons softened butter

Assorted Fillings

Light cream cheese mixed with grated cucumber and
   minced dill weed
Peanut butter and jam
Mashed banana and peanut butter
Sliced pickles and minced ham mixed with light cream
   cheese and a few drops of milk
Light cream cheese, thinly sliced tomatoes, and basil leaves
Drained crushed pineapple or chutney and light cream
   cheese

1. Remove crusts from bread and cut loaves into thin slices. Scrape a thin layer of butter on each slice of bread, add fillings of choice, and then be creative in how you put them together.

2. Wrap sandwiches in plastic wrap and store in the refrigerator until tea time.

Sandwich Assembly Ideas

- Make sandwiches with three slices of bread and two layers of filling.
- Cut sandwiches into small pieces, either in three strips, or four quarters.
- Cut sandwiches with animal cookie cutters and stand them up on the plate to make "Zoowiches."
- Make interesting shapes with any kind of cookie cutter.

Lemon Soup

The orzo (a tiny, rice-sized semolina pasta) and broth can be prepared in advance and the eggs added at the last minutes for this light, refreshing soup.

Preparation Time: 30 minutes • Serves 8

5 cups rich chicken broth
3 cups water
½ cup orzo
4 egg whites
2 egg yolks
Juice of 2 lemons

1. In a large saucepan or kettle bring the broth and water to a boil. Add the orzo and cook over medium heat for 15–20 minutes until the pasta is tender but not soggy.

2. In a large bowl beat the egg whites with 2 tablespoons water until soft peaks form.

3. In a separate bowl beat the egg yolks with the lemon juice; fold into the egg whites.

4. Add some of the hot broth to the egg mixture and stir gently to warm up the egg. Return all the egg mixture to the hot broth and simmer, stirring constantly until the soup thickens slightly. Serve at once.

Braised Lamb with Vegetables

This casserole can be made ahead and reheated. It only gets better.

Preparation Time: 20 minutes • Cooking Time: 1½ hours • Serves 8

2 pounds lean, boneless lamb breast and neck meat
   (or lamb stew meat), cut into 1-inch cubes and trimmed
   of fat
¼ cup flour
¼ teaspoon salt
¼ teaspoon freshly ground pepper
1 tablespoon canola oil
1 tablespoon sugar
4 cloves garlic, mashed
1 teaspoon dried thyme
3 large ripe tomatoes, chopped with liquid and seeds
   reserved
3 sprigs parsley, tied together
Salt and freshly ground pepper
1½ cups hot water
4 medium potatoes, peeled and halved
2 tablespoons minced fresh parsley

1. Dredge the lamb in flour by placing it in a paper bag with the flour, salt, and pepper and shaking until the chunks of lamb are thoroughly coated.

2. Heat the oil in a Dutch oven and sauté the lamb over medium heat until brown on all sides. Add the sugar and cook gently while stirring.

3. Mix the garlic, thyme, and about ¼ teaspoon salt and add to the casserole. Cook for about 1 minute until the garlic softens.

4. Add the tomatoes with juice and seeds, parsley sprigs, a few gratings of pepper, and the hot water. Bring the liquid to a boil and reduce heat. Simmer very slowly for 1 hour. Taste and season with salt if needed.

5. Add the potatoes and more water if it appears dry. Continue simmering for 25 minutes, or until the meat and potatoes are tender.

6. Sprinkle with minced parsley and serve.

Baked French Fries

These are a great alternative to greasy French fries and a big hit with fast-food lovers! They are here specifically for the young folks who may not like stew.

Preparation Time: 20 minutes • Cooking Time: 20 minutes • Serves 8

6 medium Idaho potatoes
2 teaspoons canola oil
Salt and freshly ground pepper, to taste

1. Preheat oven to 400°F.
2. Peel the potatoes and cut into sticks ¼-inch square and the length of the potato. Toss potatoes with the oil in a large bowl. Use your hands to make sure all the pieces are coated with oil.
3. Spread the potatoes on a large baking sheet coated with vegetable cooking spray and bake for 20 minutes, or until the potatoes are soft on the inside and slightly browned on the outside.

Spinach Cucumber Salad with Lime Dressing

Preparation Time: 15 minutes • Serves 8

½–¾ pound fresh spinach, washed, trimmed, and spun dry
2 cucumbers, peeled and chopped
1 small red onion, thinly sliced

Dressing
Juice of 2 limes (about 3 tablespoons)
¼ teaspoon ground cumin
Salt and freshly ground pepper, to taste
1 tablespoon olive oil
½ cup plain nonfat yogurt

Arrange spinach on a platter; top with cucumbers and onion slices. Whisk together the dressing ingredients and drizzle over the salad.

Frozen Lemon Chiffon Pie

Nobody believes that this wonderfully light dessert isn't dripping with calories.

Preparation Time: 30 minutes • Freezing Time: 8 hours • Makes one 9-inch pie

Graham Cracker Crust

20 graham crackers rolled in a plastic bag or processed in food processor to a fine crumb (about 1⅓ cups)
2 tablespoons sugar
1 tablespoon water
1 tablespoon egg white, slightly beaten
2 tablespoons canola oil

Filling

¾ cup sugar
¼ cup corn syrup
2 tablespoons water
½ cup evaporated skimmed milk, very cold
3 egg whites, at room temperature (or pasteurized egg whites)
¼ cup cold orange juice
2 teaspoons grated lemon rind
Juice of 2 lemons (about ½ cup), chilled

1. Preheat oven to 350°F.

2. In a medium-size bowl combine all the crust ingredients; mix with your fingers until the crumbs are uniformly moistened. Press the crumbs into the bottom and sides of a 9-inch pie pan. Bake for 8–10 minutes, or until lightly browned. Cool on a wire rack.

3. To make the filling, mix the sugar, corn syrup, and water in a small saucepan; cook over medium heat until simmering. Cover and boil for about 1 minute. Uncover and continue simmering, without stirring, until syrup is a soft ball, 240°F, about 1–2 minutes. Remove from heat and set aside.

4. In a small chilled bowl and with chilled beaters, beat the icy cold milk until it forms peaks, but is not too stiff. Set aside.

5. Thoroughly clean the beaters. In a medium-size bowl beat the egg whites until soft peaks form. Reheat the syrup until just boiling. Continue beating egg whites on high speed while pouring the hot syrup in at a steady stream. Keep beating until mixture becomes thick, fluffy, smooth and has stiff peaks.

6. Fold in the orange juice, lemon rind, lemon juice, and whipped milk. Pile the filling into the graham cracker crust and freeze for 8 hours or overnight. Let the pie sit out for a little while to soften before slicing and serving.

Thanksgiving

Thanksgiving is a lovely holiday dedicated to sharing food with loved ones and giving thanks without all the complications of gift giving. It also presents an opportunity for cooperative cooking at its best. Larrie always offers to bring the creamed onions. Aunt Helen was a master at peeling potatoes, and for years Nana was the only one who could make the molded cranberry.

This is the meal where the "yukky" vegetables — turnips, rutabagas, winter squash, parsnips, and Brussels sprouts — get to share the limelight with the turkey. They tend to be neglected after the holiday, but are actually wonderful throughout the fall and winter. *E.S.*

~~~~~~~~~~~

Wednesday
Supper

Lentil Soup* • Crusty Bread • Applesauce

Thursday — Thanksgiving Day
Breakfast

Grapefruit • Cold Cereal • Muffins

The Dinner

Turkey with Cranberry, Apple, Sage, and Onion Stuffing*
Mashed Potatoes à la Laura*
Curried Brussels Sprouts and Cauliflower*
Baked Squash Casserole* • Creamed Onions
Golden Harvest Vegetables* • Tiny Peas
Cranberry Jelly • Crunch Top Apple Pie*
Pumpkin Pie • Mincemeat Pie

Friday
Breakfast

(even though everyone feels they will never eat again)
Fresh Fruit
Eggs of Choice • French Roast Coffee

Lunch

Turkey Sandwiches
(with sprouts, cranberry jelly, and sliced oranges)

Supper

Homemade Turkey Soup* • Crusty Bread • Leftover Pie

recipe included

THINGS TO DO AHEAD

THE WEEKEND BEFORE

- Get out the serving dishes you will need
- Begin thawing turkey, unless you have a fresh one

TUESDAY

- Make Lentil Soup, except for the spinach

WEDNESDAY

- Prepare Curried Brussels Sprouts and Cauliflower
- Prepare Baked Squash Casserole
- Cut up the Golden Harvest Vegetables
- Make Crunch Top Apple Pie

WEEKEND WORK PLAN

WEDNESDAY EVENING

- Complete Lentil Soup
- Warm bread

THURSDAY MORNING

- Prepare Turkey for oven; make Apple, Sage, and Onion Stuffing
- Set up breakfast area
- Set dinner table after breakfast

THURSDAY AFTERNOON

- Complete Golden Harvest Vegetables
- Peel and cook Mashed Potatoes (have a guest do the peeling)
- While turkey is sitting, bake the Squash Casserole and the Brussels Sprouts and Cauliflower
- Cook peas
- Warm creamed onions
- Make gravy
- Serve and enjoy one of the all-time great meals!
- Just before bed, have someone set up the coffee and juice area

FRIDAY MORNING

- Complete breakfast set-up
- Slice rest of turkey; remove meat from carcass for sandwiches
- Begin stock for Homemade Turkey Soup

FRIDAY NOON

- Set up turkey sandwich bar

FRIDAY AFTERNOON

- Strain turkey stock
- Make Homemade Turkey Soup

Lentil Soup

I add fresh spinach to many homemade soups. Kate's friend Dee first suggested how wonderful it is in lentil soup — and she was right!

Preparation Time: 20 minutes • Cooking Time: 45 minutes • Serves 8

2 cups lentils
1 clove garlic, minced
½ cup chopped celery
1 onion, chopped
1 cup chopped carrot
½ pound kielbasa, or other sausage
1 teaspoon dried thyme
6 cups water
2½ cups peeled and chopped tomatoes
½ teaspoon salt
Freshly ground pepper, to taste
1 tablespoon brown sugar
1 tablespoon lemon juice
1 tablespoon red wine vinegar
4 cups fresh spinach, washed and shredded

1. Rinse and pick over lentils.
2. In a large, covered kettle steam the garlic, celery, onion, and carrots in 2 tablespoons water over low heat until the vegetables are tender, about 10 minutes.
3. Slice the sausage and brown in a skillet. Drain and pat the sausage with paper towel to remove excess fat.
4. Add sausage and lentils to the kettle with the water and thyme. Bring to a boil, turn down heat, cover, and simmer for 30 minutes, until the lentils are tender.
5. Uncover and add the tomatoes, salt, pepper, brown sugar, lemon juice, vinegar, and spinach; simmer for an additional 15 minutes, stirring occasionally. Serve piping hot.

Cranberry, Apple, Sage, and Onion Stuffing

I am a great believer in making things from scratch — with a few exceptions. One of these is turkey stuffing. Pepperidge Farm Herbed Stuffing Mix is delicious as is or with some embellishment.

Preparation Time: 15 minutes • Makes 8 cups (enough to stuff a 12-pound turkey)

8 cups herbed stuffing mix
2 stalks celery, chopped
1 large onion, chopped
4 apples, peeled, cored, and chopped
1½ teaspoons rubbed sage
1 teaspoon dried thyme
½ teaspoon salt
¼ teaspoon freshly ground pepper
1 cup chopped cranberries
2 tablespoons unsalted butter
1½ cups water

1. Just before you are ready to roast your turkey, begin making the stuffing. Place the stuffing mix in a very large bowl. Add the celery, onion, apples, sage, thyme, salt, pepper, and cranberries. Mix well with a large wooden spoon or your hands.

2. Heat the butter in the water and pour over the stuffing mix; stir lightly with a fork.

3. Loosely pack the cavity of the turkey before putting it into the oven. Cook turkey according to directions on the wrapping, or use your favorite method. Put any extra stuffing in a casserole dish and bake with the turkey for the last hour.

Note: To avoid bacterial growth (which can possibly cause illness), stuff the turkey just before cooking and pack it loosely in the cavity.

Mashed Potatoes à la Laura

Laura, a friend of Kate's from Idaho, has been at several of our recent Thanksgiving dinners and taken charge of potato mashing. Our mashed potatoes have never been as smooth and creamy as when Laura makes them. Her tips are: (1) be sure the potato cooking liquid is evaporated and the potatoes well mashed before adding anything to them; (2) heat the milk before adding it to the potatoes, and (3) grow up in Idaho.

Preparation Time: 30 minutes • Serves 8

8 medium-size mature potatoes, peeled and cut in half
1–3 tablespoons butter
½ cup hot milk
Salt and freshly ground pepper, to taste

1. Add the potatoes to a large pot of boiling, salted water and cook for about 20 minutes, or until they are tender when pierced with a fork. Pour off the water and save it for making gravy if you are so inclined.

2. Over very low heat mash the potatoes with a potato masher until they seem quite dry. Add the butter and hot milk; mash and beat with a potato masher until they are smooth and creamy. Place the potatoes in a special serving dish and serve at once — since that's when they are best. If you must wait, balance the potato pot over a kettle of simmering water until ready to serve.

Curried Brussels Sprouts and Cauliflower

This is a delightful way to indulge in those healthy cruciferous vegetables. It can be prepared ahead and cooked along with the turkey.

Preparation Time: 30 minutes • Baking Time: 45 minutes • Serves 12

1½ pounds brussels sprouts, or two 10-ounce packages frozen
1 head cauliflower, cleaned and cut into 1-inch cauliflowerets
Up to 2 cups evaporated skimmed milk
2 tablespoons cornstarch
¼ cup half-and-half
2 teaspoons curry powder or combination of suitable spices
1 cup light sour cream or plain nonfat yogurt or a combination of the two
1 teaspoon butter
Salt and freshly ground pepper, to taste

1. Preheat oven to 350°F (or cook along with the turkey).
2. Steam vegetables until tender crisp.
3. Combine some of the liquid used for steaming with enough milk to make 2 cups and pour it all into a medium-size saucepan. Mix the cornstarch with ¼ cup cold milk and pour into the saucepan.
4. Cook over medium heat stirring constantly until the mixture boils and thickens. Add the half-and-half. Remove from heat and stir in curry powder, sour cream or yogurt, butter, and salt and pepper, to taste.
5. Arrange the vegetables in a shallow 2-quart baking dish and pour the sauce over them. Bake for 45 minutes until bubbly. Serve hot.

Baked Squash Casserole

This dish can be prepared ahead and baked alongside the turkey.

Preparation time: 15 minutes • Baking Time: 30–40 minutes • Serves 8

4 cups cooked winter squash, butternut or hubbard
1 tablespoon butter, softened
3 tablespoons brown sugar
¼ cup plain nonfat yogurt
½ teaspoon salt
¼ teaspoon nutmeg
1 egg, slightly beaten
½ cup chopped toasted almonds (reserve 2 tablespoons for topping)

1. Preheat oven to 350°F.
2. Mix all ingredients, except the almonds for topping, thoroughly but not excessively. Pour into a 2-quart casserole coated with vegetable cooking spray, top with reserved almonds, and bake for 30–40 minutes until bubbly.

Tip: Chop almonds and spread them on the tray of a toaster oven. Set temperature for 400°F and toast for 5–10 minutes, until they are golden brown.

Golden Harvest Vegetables

This is a prime yukky vegetable recipe which has been a favorite on our Thanksgiving table for years. The vegetables can be cut and cooked in advance and reheated and glazed just before serving.

Preparation Time: 45 minutes • Serves 12

1 pound carrots
1 pound parsnips
1 pound rutabaga (yellow turnip)

Glaze

3 tablespoons butter
2 tablespoons fresh lemon juice
2 tablespoons real maple syrup or brown sugar
¼ teaspoon cinnamon
½ teapoon salt
Freshly ground pepper, to taste

1. Peel and cut all the vegetables into 3 by ¼-inch sticks. Steam them until tender crisp — about 8 minutes for the carrots and rutabagas, less for the parsnips.

2. In a small saucepan, over low heat, warm the butter, lemon juice, maple syrup, cinnamon, and salt until well blended.

3. Pour the glaze over the hot vegetables; toss gently and serve.

Crunch Top Apple Pie

Preparation Time: 30 minutes • Baking Time: 40–50 minutes • Makes one 9-inch pie

One 9-inch pie shell, unbaked
6 tart baking apples, peeled, cored, and sliced
1 cup plain nonfat yogurt
1 egg, beaten
½ cup sugar
¼ cup all-purpose flour

Topping

¼ cup butter, melted
⅓ cup granulated sugar
⅓ cup brown sugar
½ cup flour
1 teaspoon cinnamon
½ cup chopped walnuts

1. Preheat oven to 450°F.
2. In a large bowl toss the apples with the yogurt, egg, sugar, and flour until well coated.
3. Pour the apple mixture into the pie shell and bake for 10 minutes. Turn the oven down to 350°F and bake for 35–40 minutes.
4. Mix the topping ingredients together and sprinkle over the pie. Bake an additional 15–20 minutes until the topping looks crunchy. Cool the pie on a wire rack.

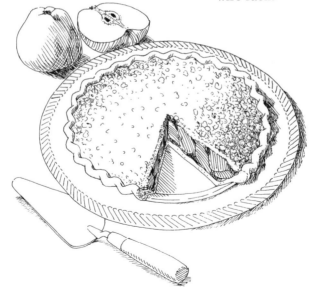

Homemade Turkey Soup

I get compulsive about making turkey soup because I can't bear to throw away the carcass. The rich stock makes an excellent soup, and excess stock can be stored in the freezer for another time.

Preparation Time: 20 minutes • Serves 8

2 quarts turkey stock
2 cups turkey meat, cut into 1-inch chunks
Leftover harvest vegetables, cut into 1-inch pieces, and
   leftover mashed potatoes *or* 2 carrots, peeled and sliced,
   and 2 large potatoes, peeled and cut into ½-inch chunks
   and partially cooked in the microwave
1 teaspoon tarragon
1 cup shredded fresh spinach
Salt and pepper to taste

1. Place stock, turkey, vegetables, and tarragon in large kettle. Bring to a boil; reduce heat and simmer until everything is hot, about 15 minutes.
2. Add spinach; adjust seasoning to taste and cook for 5 minutes, until spinach is wilted. Serve hot.

Turkey Stock
Preparation Time: 5 hours • Makes 6–8 quarts

1 turkey carcass with stuffing and meat removed and saved
   (Save all skin, bone, and drippings for the stockpot as well.)
1 onion, cut in quarters
1 bay leaf
10 peppercorns
1 teaspoon salt
1 cup celery leaves
1 sprig parsley
8–10 quarts water
1 very large stockpot or kettle

1. Place all the ingredients in a very large stockpot or kettle. The water should almost cover the bones.
2. Bring to a boil, cover, reduce heat, and simmer for 5 hours.
3. Strain stock into large bowls and store in the refrigerator until fat congeals. Remove fat and store stock in 1 quart freezer containers until ready to use.

Converting Recipe Measurements to Metric

Use the following formulas for converting U.S. measurements to metric. Since the conversions are not exact, it's important to convert the measurements for all of the ingredients to maintain the same proportions as the original recipe.

When The Measurement Given Is	Multiply It By	To Convert To
teaspoons	4.93	milliliters
tablespoons	14.79	milliliters
fluid ounces	29.57	milliliters
cups	236.59	milliliters
cups	.236	liters
pints	473.18	milliliters
pints	.473	liters
quarts	946.36	milliliters
quarts	.946	liters
gallons	3.785	liters
ounces	28.35	grams
pounds	.454	kilograms
inches	2.54	centimeters
degrees Fahrenheit	$\frac{5}{9}$ (temperature − 32)	degrees Celsius (Centigrade)

INDEX